The Badass Mom

Guided Story Journal

The Badass

Guided Story Journal

A Memory Book for Her

Amazing Life Stories

Jed Smith

TorchOwl Library

Published by TorchOwl Library

ISBN: 979-8-9939274-1-1

AI Assistance Notice: Portions of this journal's prompts and guidance were developed with the assistance of artificial intelligence tools to ensure comprehensive coverage of life experiences and effective question formulation.

Third-Party Quotations: Brief quotations from various authors throughout this journal are used for inspirational purposes under the principle of fair use and are properly attributed to their respective sources.

Content Advisory: This journal contains prompts addressing mature themes and life experiences that may include sensitive topics. Users should exercise discretion in what they choose to explore and share.

Disclaimer: This legacy journal is intended for personal reflection, memory preservation, and storytelling. It is not a substitute for professional genealogical research, legal documentation, or historical verification. The prompts and guidance provided are designed to encourage honest, meaningful reflection and should be used at the writer's own discretion. The author and publisher assume no responsibility for how the content of this journal is shared or interpreted by others.

All memories, stories, and reflections recorded in this journal are the personal expressions of the writer and represent their individual perspective and recollection.

A Word from the Author

I created this journal because I bought my mom a legacy journal hoping she'd fill it out. After months of it sitting untouched on the piano, I picked it up one afternoon while visiting and started reading through the prompts. A few were somewhat interesting, but I immediately understood why it remained blank. It read like a genealogy assignment, not an invitation. A trip to the dentist, not down memory lane.

If my mom had opened it and found prompts that genuinely intrigued her—questions that tickled her memory in a fun, compelling way—I'm certain she would have filled out that first "Memory Spark." Then another. And while she might not relate to every prompt in this book (not all women have lived the same experiences), I would treasure reading whatever memories, stories, lessons, and wisdom she chose to share.

Some women prefer safe, traditional questions because they allow them to document the exact kind of lives they've lived. And there's nothing wrong with that. But for others, sitting down to write about genealogical timelines and milestones their children already know about isn't an interesting or compelling way to spend their time. What excites them is sharing the story of how she and her best friends put the old car in neutral, rolled it down the street, popped the clutch, and cruised off into the night for a two-hour joyride before sneaking back into the house feeling like rebel queens.

Of the three women I cherish most in this world, two have passed on. I no longer have the opportunity to read what they might have chosen to share based on the Memory Sparks in this journal. My purpose in creating it was simple: to make something so interesting that my mom would enjoy spending time with it each night as much as tending her garden or decorating her home for the upcoming holiday. Not because she felt obligated, but because she genuinely wanted to.

That's how interesting I've attempted to make these prompts. If the woman in your life has lived boldly, authentically, and on her own terms, this journal was made for her.

How To Use

This journal is designed to be simple, flexible, and entirely yours. Each section follows the same structure, so once you understand the flow, you can move through it at your own pace—and in any order you choose.

So go ahead and flip through it, read the titles, and start with whatever grabs your attention first. This isn't a book you have to complete front to back. It's a collection of 60 Memory Sparks, and you get to decide which ones are worth your time. (Actually, it's 63—I couldn't quite get it whittled down to 60)

Start by reading the Memory Spark. Each one is a short, 3-4 paragraph passage that sets the scene and gets your memories flowing around a specific subject. It's not a lesson—it's a spark designed to stir something in you, to help you remember moments you might not have thought about in years.

Next, review the six prompt questions and choose one (or several, if you'd like) to explore. The key here is to be bold, open, and make no effort to write perfectly. The only perfect page is a blank page, and those will do nothing to help you record and relive your memories—and nothing for your loved ones who want to read them someday to know you on a completely different, more intimate level.

If a memory is right on the tip of your tongue but won't come, move on. Plant the seed in your mind—"it will come to me"—and when it does (in the shower, driving, washing dishes), grab your phone or a piece of paper and note it. Not every memory recalls on demand, and that's okay. This isn't an assignment with a deadline. This isn't a task to be completed. This is something that should be fun, and when you approach it that way, that vibe will come through in what you write.

If a Memory Spark doesn't resonate with you, skip it. If it's something you haven't experienced, skip it. There's a reason there are 63 prompts in this journal. You're not going to identify with every experience. The idea was to provide you with enough inspiration to end up with 30 or 40 recorded memories. That will be a resounding success. That's thirty or forty more stories you and your family have to share than if you hadn't done it at all.

It's really that simple: Read the Memory Spark, review the prompt questions, and go wherever they take you in the two wide-ruled pages that follow. Write as much or as little as you want. Skip prompts that don't resonate. Come back to ones that do. This journal is a treat, not a test. Use it however it serves you best.

Memory Sparks

Youth & Rebellion (15-52)

Relationships & Love (53-82)

Memory Sparks

Identity & Transformation (83-120)

Motherhood (121-158)

Memory Sparks

Defiance & Standing Up (159-196)

Risk & Adventure (197-222)

Memory Sparks

Body & Physicality (223-248)

Money & Power (249-262)

Survival & Lessons (263-284)

Youth & Rebellion

9 Memory Sparks

Your Wildest Night

"Life is either a daring adventure or nothing at all."
— Helen Keller

There are nights that blur at the edges, and then there's the one that refuses to fade no matter how many years pass. The night that became legend—the story you've told a hundred times and still can't quite believe happened. Maybe it started innocently enough: dinner with friends, a concert that was supposed to end at midnight, a party someone said would be "chill." But then someone suggested something, someone else said yes, and suddenly you were in motion, making decisions that seemed brilliant at 2 a.m. and questionable by dawn.

The details are what make it unforgettable. The sequence of events that sounds fabricated but isn't. The person who showed up out of nowhere. The moment everything went sideways in the best possible way. The near-miss with disaster. The thing you still can't believe you did, but multiple witnesses confirm absolutely happened. Maybe you were dancing on tables, or driving to another state on a whim, or doing something so out of character that people who know you now wouldn't recognize the person you were that night.

That night didn't just happen to you—you happened to that night. You were bold, reckless, fully alive. Maybe you woke up somewhere unexpected, or had to piece the story together from friends' accounts, or came home just as the sun was rising with your shoes in your hand and mascara smeared. Maybe there were consequences, or maybe it was just crazy, innocent fun.

Some nights are designed to be wild. Others just turn that way when nobody's looking. This is the story your kids will say "You did WHAT?" Let them hear it.

Writing Prompt Questions

1. What was the plan for that night, and when did it go completely off script? Where were you supposed to be, and where did you actually end up? What was the turning point?

2. Who were you with, and who was the ringleader? Was there one person who led the charge, or did you all collectively lose your minds together? What role did you play in the chaos?

3. What's the moment from that night that people still bring up? The thing you did, the thing that happened, the line someone said? What's the detail that makes the story unforgettable?

4. Was there a moment when you thought "This could go very wrong" but kept going anyway? What was happening, and what made you decide the risk was worth it?

5. How did the night end? Did you make it home? Wake up somewhere unexpected? Have to piece together what happened from other people's versions? What was the aftermath?

6. If you could go back to that night, would you do it again exactly the same way? What do you wish you'd done differently, or is it perfect as a memory precisely because you can't do it again?

Breaking the Rules

"The question isn't who is going to let me; it's who is going to stop me."
— Ayn Rand

There's a difference between breaking a rule by accident and breaking one on purpose. The second kind requires intention. You knew what you weren't supposed to do, weighed the consequences, and decided to do it anyway. Maybe you were mad, or curious, or just tired of being told no. Maybe the rule seemed ridiculous and you wanted to prove it. Maybe you broke it just to see if you could get away with it.

These are the rules that felt personal—the curfew that was too early, the dress code that made no sense, the expectation that you'd go along with something you fundamentally disagreed with. Maybe it was your parents' rule, or the school's, or society's. Maybe it was spoken or unspoken, but either way, you knew exactly what line you were crossing when you stepped over it.

What makes these stories interesting isn't just the rule you broke, but why you broke it. What were you standing up for? What were you rebelling against? Were you trying to prove something to someone else, or just to yourself? And what happened when you did it—did the sky fall, or did you discover the rule was more bark than bite?

Some rules deserve to be broken. Some don't, but you broke them anyway and learned something in the process. Either way, the moment you decided "I'm doing this regardless" says something about who you were becoming. This is the story of a line you crossed on purpose, and what you found on the other side.

Maybe you got caught and faced consequences that taught you boundaries have teeth. Or maybe you got away with it and realized that some rules only have power if you give it to them. Either way, you made a choice that day to prioritize your own judgment over someone else's authority.

Writing Prompt Questions

1. What rule did you break, and who made that rule? Was it your parents, your school, your church, society? What did the rule say you couldn't do, and why did it feel wrong or unfair to you?

2. What made you decide to break it? Was it a moment of rebellion, a test of courage, or standing up for something you believed in?

3. How did you break the rule—did you do it quietly or make a statement? Did you sneak around, or did you break it right out in the open? Who knew what you were doing?

4. What did it feel like in the moment you broke the rule? Were you scared, exhilarated, defiant? Did it feel like freedom or like you'd just made a huge mistake?

5. Did you get caught, and if so, what happened? What were the consequences, and were they worth it? Or did you get away with it and never face any fallout?

6. Looking back now, do you think breaking that rule was the right call? Would you do it again? What did breaking it teach you about yourself, authority, or what really matters?

Getting Caught Red-Handed

"I'd rather regret the things I've done than regret the things I haven't done."
— Lucille Ball

There's no feeling quite like being caught in the act. Not suspected, not questioned later, but caught—mid-action, undeniable, with no time to come up with a story or hide the evidence. Someone walks in, looks up, turns around, or shows up at exactly the wrong moment, and suddenly you're standing there with absolutely no way to explain yourself. The thing you were doing, the place you weren't supposed to be, the person you weren't supposed to be with—all of it exposed in an instant.

Maybe you were somewhere you'd snuck into, doing something you'd been explicitly told not to do, or with someone you'd sworn you weren't seeing. Maybe you were stealing something, breaking a rule, lying about where you were, or in a compromising position that required zero explanation because it was immediately, painfully obvious what was happening. The moment of eye contact when you both realize they know and you know they know—that moment before anyone speaks—is burned into your memory forever.

What happened next depended on who caught you and what you were doing. Maybe you tried to lie anyway, even though it was hopeless. Maybe you just froze. Maybe you laughed nervously or tried to run. Maybe the person who caught you was angrier than you expected, or surprisingly calm, or deeply disappointed in a way that felt worse than yelling.

Getting caught red-handed is humbling, mortifying, and sometimes hilarious in hindsight. Maybe there were consequences that taught you about accountability, or maybe you somehow talked your way out of it despite the evidence being irrefutable. Either way, that moment when you had absolutely no excuse changed something. You learned that actions have witnesses, that secrets don't always stay secret, and that sometimes the truth catches up faster than you can outrun it.

Writing Prompt Questions

1. What were you doing when you got caught, and who caught you? Set the scene: where were you, what were you in the middle of, and who walked in or showed up?

2. What was the exact moment you realized you'd been caught? Was it eye contact, a gasp, someone saying your name? Describe that split second when you knew there was no escape.

3. What did you say or do in that moment? Did you freeze, try to lie, laugh it off, or immediately confess? What was your instinct?

4. How did the person who caught you react? Were they angry, shocked, disappointed, or weirdly calm? What did they say or do, and how did you respond?

5. What were the consequences of getting caught? Grounded, fired, dumped, punished? Or did you somehow escape with a warning? How bad was the fallout?

6. Looking back, is it funny now, or does it still make you cringe? Can you laugh about it, or does the memory still sting? Would you do it again knowing you'd get caught, or was the humiliation enough to learn your lesson?

The Bet or Dare

"Fortune favors the bold."
— Virgil

There's something about a dare that bypasses every rational thought in your brain. Someone says "I bet you won't..." and suddenly you're committed, not because you want to do the thing, but because you refuse to be the person who backs down. Maybe it was jumping off something too high, kissing someone you shouldn't have, stealing something ridiculous, or doing something outrageous in public. Maybe it was stupid, reckless, or borderline dangerous. You did it anyway.

The best dares come with an audience. Friends watching, waiting to see if you'll actually go through with it. The moment before you commit—when you're weighing whether this is worth it—everyone can see the calculation happening on your face. And then you decide. You jump, you kiss, you run, you do the thing, and suddenly you're the person who actually did it. The legend who didn't chicken out.

What happened after is the real story. Maybe it went perfectly and you became a hero for the night. Maybe it went sideways and you had to deal with consequences you didn't anticipate. Maybe you got hurt, got caught, or got exactly what you deserved for taking a dare that stupid. Or maybe nothing bad happened at all, and you walked away with a story that proved you had guts.

Some dares are harmless fun. Others are the kind of decisions you look back on and think "I'm lucky I survived that." Either way, the dare itself wasn't really about the task—it was about proving something. Proving you weren't scared, weren't boring, weren't someone who played it safe. The dare was a test, and you passed it, even if passing meant doing something absolutely ridiculous. This is the story of the time someone dared you, and you couldn't say no.

Writing Prompt Questions

1. What was the dare or bet, and who challenged you? What exactly did they say you wouldn't do, and why did that make you determined to prove them wrong?

2. Where were you, and who was watching? Was this in front of friends, strangers, or someone you were trying to impress? Set the scene.

3. What was going through your mind in the moment before you did it? Were you scared, excited, or just too proud to back down? What made you actually commit?

4. What happened when you did it? Did it go as planned, or did something unexpected happen? Walk us through the actual moment you followed through.

5. What were the consequences—immediate or later? Did you get in trouble, get hurt, or get away clean? How did people react?

6. Looking back, was it worth it? Do you regret taking the dare, or are you glad you proved you had the guts to do it? What did that moment teach you about yourself?

Road Trip with Friends

"Not all who wander are lost."
— J.R.R. Tolkien

There's something about a road trip that feels like freedom in its purest form. Windows down, music loud, nowhere you have to be and nobody telling you what to do. Maybe it was planned for weeks with maps and reservations, or maybe someone said "let's just go" and you were in the car twenty minutes later. Either way, once you were on the road, the destination mattered less than the fact that you were moving, together, toward something that felt like possibility.

The best road trips aren't about where you ended up—they're about what happened along the way. The breakdown in the middle of nowhere. The detour that turned into the highlight. The motel that was so sketchy you laughed about it for years. The conversation at 3 a.m. when someone finally said what they'd been holding back. The song that came on at exactly the right moment and became the soundtrack to that entire summer. The inside jokes that only make sense if you were there.

Road trips reveal people. You learn who's good in a crisis, who can't read a map to save their life, who gets cranky when they're hungry, and who's willing to sleep in the car to save money. You learn who you can spend seventy-two hours with in close quarters and still like at the end. You make decisions together, get lost together, survive on gas station snacks together, and come home with stories that sound exaggerated but aren't.

That road trip wasn't just about the miles—it was about the people in the car and the version of yourself you became when you left everything familiar behind. You were braver on the road, funnier, more spontaneous. You said yes to things you'd normally overthink. This is the story of the road trip that became a benchmark for every adventure that came after.

Writing Prompt Questions

1. Where were you going, and whose idea was it? Was this planned or spontaneous? What made you decide to go, and who was in the car with you?

2. What car were you driving, and what was the vibe? Describe the vehicle, the music, the snacks, the chaos. What made this trip feel different from just driving somewhere?

3. What unexpected thing happened on the road? A breakdown, a detour, getting lost, meeting someone random? What's the moment that turned into the story you still tell?

4. What conversation happened on that trip that you still remember? Was there a 3 a.m. heart-to-heart, a confession, or something someone said that changed how you saw them?

5. What was the best part—a specific stop, a view, a moment, or just being together? What made this trip unforgettable beyond the destination?

6. How did that road trip change your friendships or change you? Did you come back different? What did you learn about yourself or the people you traveled with?

Sneaking Out

"Adventure is worthwhile in itself."
— Amelia Earhart

There's a particular kind of adrenaline that comes with sneaking out of the house after everyone's asleep. Your heart hammering in your chest. The careful navigation of creaky floorboards. Choosing the best window or door. The moment you're finally outside in the night air, free and terrified and absolutely alive all at the same time. Sneaking out wasn't just about where you were going—it was about getting out of the house undetected and why you wanted to.

You knew your family's rhythm well enough to know when the best time would be to make your move. Maybe your parents watched The Tonight Show and would be asleep within a half hour of it ending. It's even possible you rehearsed your escape during the day when no one was watching, making sure the route you had chosen had no undiscovered squeaks. You may have even lubricated the hinges of a door with a little WD-40. The logistics of silently exiting the house weren't an afterthought—they were part of the whole experience.

But the real story is what happened after. Where were you going? A party? To meet someone? Just driving around because you could? Who was waiting for you? What did freedom taste like at two in the morning when you were young and, as far as you were concerned, invincible?

Some of the best stories start with "So I climbed out my bedroom window..." The hatching of a plan. The clean escape. The journey to your destination. What happened when you got there. The trip back. Whether you got caught or came away unscathed. This is the story that makes your kids say "You did WHAT?" The night you chose adventure over obedience, and the memory of feeling absolutely free, even if just for a few hours.

Writing Prompt Questions

1. Where were you going that night, and why was it worth the risk of sneaking out? What was waiting for you that couldn't wait until morning?

2. Walk us through the actual escape—what time was it, what route did you take, and what obstacles did you have to navigate? Did you have a system or was it improvised?

3. What were you wearing, and did you have to change clothes once you got outside? Were you dressed for stealth or for wherever you were headed?

4. Tell us about the moment you were finally outside and free. What did that feel like? What were you thinking as you walked or drove away from your house?

5. Did you get caught—either that night or later? If yes, how did your parents find out and what was the fallout? If no, how did you pull off the perfect crime?

6. Who else was involved in this adventure, and are they still in your life? What role did they play, and do you still talk about that night?

The Prank That Went Too Far

"Life is too important to be taken seriously."
— Oscar Wilde

Most pranks are harmless—a little mischief, some laughs, everyone moves on. But then there's the one that crossed a line you didn't see coming. It started as a joke, something funny that would give everyone a good story. And then it escalated. Maybe someone took it further than planned, or the target didn't think it was funny, or the consequences spiraled beyond anyone's control. What was supposed to be hilarious became something else entirely.

The best pranks require planning. You had to think it through, get people on board, coordinate timing. Maybe you were TPing a house, moving furniture, setting up an elaborate scheme, or playing a trick that seemed brilliant until it wasn't. The execution felt flawless. Everyone was laughing. And then the moment happened—the moment you realized this had gone too far and there was no taking it back.

Maybe someone got genuinely hurt or upset. Maybe property got damaged in ways you didn't anticipate. Maybe authorities got involved when you thought it would stay between friends. Maybe the person you pranked didn't laugh it off—they got angry, or humiliated, or betrayed. The prank that was supposed to bring people together ended up doing the opposite.

What happened after the prank went wrong is the real story. Did you own up to it or try to hide? Did you apologize or double down? Did friendships survive, or did this become the thing that ended them? And what did you learn about the difference between funny and cruel, between harmless fun and genuine harm? Some pranks become legendary for being perfectly executed. Others become legendary for going spectacularly, unforgettably wrong. This is the story of the second kind.

Writing Prompt Questions

1. What was the prank, and whose idea was it? What were you trying to accomplish, and who was the target? Set up what was supposed to happen.

2. How did you plan and execute it? Who was involved, what did each person do, and how long did it take to set up? Walk us through the preparation.

3. What was the exact moment you realized it had gone too far? What happened that made you think "oh no, this isn't funny anymore"?

4. How did the target react? Were they angrier than you expected, more hurt, or did they handle it differently than you thought they would? What did they say or do?

5. What were the consequences? Did you get in trouble, have to make amends, face punishment? How did you deal with the fallout?

6. Looking back, do you regret it, or was it a valuable lesson learned the hard way? What did that prank teach you about boundaries, humor, or how your actions affect other people?

Getting Suspended or Expelled

"I have never let my schooling interfere with my education."
— Mark Twain

Getting suspended or expelled isn't something that happens by accident. You don't wake up one day and find yourself banned from school for no reason. There's a buildup—warnings ignored, rules broken, a final incident that made someone in authority decide you'd crossed the line one too many times. Maybe you deserved it. Maybe the punishment didn't fit the crime. Either way, the day you got the news that you were officially out was a defining moment.

What got you kicked out says something about who you were then. Maybe it was fighting, skipping too many classes, talking back to the wrong person, or getting caught doing something you thought you'd get away with. Maybe it was one spectacular mistake, or maybe it was the culmination of smaller rebellions that finally added up. Maybe you'd been pushing boundaries all year, testing how far you could go before someone pushed back. And then they did.

The worst part wasn't necessarily the suspension or expulsion itself—it was telling your parents. That conversation is seared into memory. The disappointment, the anger, the lecture, the consequences that extended far beyond whatever the school decided. Or maybe your parents surprised you. Maybe they fought for you, or understood, or were too tired to care. Either way, you had to face the fact that your actions had blown up in a way you couldn't undo.

Getting kicked out of school forced you to reckon with consequences in a way nothing else had. Maybe it was a wake-up call that straightened you out. Maybe it was proof that the system was broken and you were better off somewhere else. Maybe it derailed everything for a while, or maybe it redirected you toward something better. Either way, you survived it.

Writing Prompt Questions

1. What did you do that got you suspended or expelled? Walk us through the incident or pattern of behavior that finally crossed the line. What was the final straw?

2. How did you find out? Were you called to the principal's office, sent a letter, told by someone else? What was that moment like when you learned the decision?

3. What was going through your mind when it happened? Were you shocked, defiant, scared, or did you see it coming? How did you react?

4. How did you tell your parents, and what was their reaction? Did they punish you further, defend you, or were they surprisingly understanding? What was that conversation like?

5. What were the consequences beyond the suspension or expulsion? Did you have to change schools, repeat a grade, lose privileges? How did it affect your life at the time?

6. Looking back, was getting kicked out deserved, or was it an overreaction? What did that experience teach you about authority, consequences, or yourself? Did it change your trajectory?

Skipping School

"The only time my education was interrupted was when I was in school."
— George Bernard Shaw

There's a difference between being sick and staying home, and deciding on a Tuesday morning that you're just not going to school today. Real skipping requires intention. You weighed the risks, calculated whether you'd get caught, and decided that whatever you were going to do instead was worth it. Maybe you forged a note, faked sick convincingly enough that your parents believed you, or just walked out mid-day when no one was paying attention.

The best part about skipping wasn't avoiding school—it was the freedom of being somewhere you weren't supposed to be during hours when everyone else was trapped in class. Maybe you went to the movies at 11 a.m., drove to the beach, hung out at someone's house whose parents worked, or just wandered around town feeling like you'd gotten away with something. The world felt different on a weekday morning when you were supposed to be in third period. Everything was quieter, emptier, and entirely yours.

But skipping always came with the risk of getting caught. Maybe you ran into someone's parent at the mall, or a teacher saw you somewhere you shouldn't be, or the school called home and you hadn't covered your tracks well enough. Maybe you got busted and faced consequences, or maybe you executed the perfect skip and no one ever knew. Either way, the adrenaline of doing something you absolutely weren't supposed to do made even boring activities feel like an adventure.

Skipping school was a small rebellion, a test of whether you could outsmart the system. Some days you skipped because you needed a break. Other days you skipped because someone talked you into it, or because you wanted to prove you could. This is the story of the day you chose freedom over attendance.

Writing Prompt Questions

1. Why did you skip school that day? Was it planned ahead of time, or a spontaneous decision? What made you decide this particular day was worth the risk?

2. How did you pull it off? Did you forge a note, fake being sick, sneak out, or have a parent who didn't ask questions? Walk us through your strategy.

3. What did you do instead of going to school? Where did you go, who were you with, and what made it worth skipping? Describe how you spent those stolen hours.

4. Was there a close call or moment when you thought you might get caught? Did you see someone you knew, or almost get busted? What happened?

5. Did you get caught, and if so, how? Did the school call home, did someone see you, or did you confess? What were the consequences?

6. Looking back, was it worth it? Do you remember what you missed at school that day, or do you only remember what you did instead? Would you skip again if you could go back?

Relationships & Love

7 Memory Sparks

The Proposal

"Marriage is a partnership of equals."
— Ruth Bader Ginsburg

Marriage proposals are supposed to be fairy tales—down on one knee, candlelight, rose petals, the perfect romantic moment you've been dreaming about since you were a kid. But real proposals are rarely that simple. Maybe yours was romantic and perfect, or maybe it was awkward, surprising, hilarious, or nothing like what you imagined. Maybe you saw it coming from a mile away, or maybe it blindsided you completely. Either way, the moment someone asked you to spend forever with them changed everything.

The details matter. Where were you—somewhere fancy or somewhere completely ordinary? Was it public or private? Did they have a speech planned or did they fumble through it? Was the ring what you expected, or a total surprise? Did you cry, laugh, or just stand there in shock trying to process what was happening? And most importantly—did you say yes immediately, or did you hesitate for even a second?

Some proposals are grand gestures that involve planning, coordination, and an audience. Others happen in a quiet moment when someone just can't wait anymore and asks right then, unplanned and unrehearsed. Some are exactly what you wanted. Others are so awkward or unexpected that you laugh about them forever. The proposal itself is just the question, but how it was asked says something about who was asking and what kind of marriage you were about to build.

That moment—when you became engaged, when forever became a real plan instead of an abstract idea—was a turning point. Maybe you knew instantly it was right. Maybe you had doubts you pushed down. Maybe it was the beginning of the best decision you ever made, or maybe it was the start of something more complicated. Either way, this is the story of how someone asked and what you answered.

Writing Prompt Questions

1. Where were you when the proposal happened, and what were you doing? Set the scene—was it planned and romantic, or spontaneous and unexpected?

2. How did they ask? Was there a speech, a ring, a grand gesture? Did it go smoothly or was it awkward? Walk us through exactly what happened.

3. What was your immediate reaction? Did you say yes right away, or were you shocked into silence? What were you thinking and feeling in that moment?

4. Who knew about it beforehand—did they ask your parents, tell friends, plan with others? Or was it a complete secret until it happened?

5. What happened immediately after? Did you call people, celebrate, or just sit there trying to process it? How did the rest of that day or night unfold?

6. Looking back now, what do you remember most about that moment? Is it still a cherished memory, or does it feel different now than it did then? What does that proposal represent about your relationship?

The Heartbreak

"Hearts will never be practical until they are made unbreakable."
— L. Frank Baum

Not all heartbreaks are created equal. Some you get over in a few weeks. Others crack you open and rearrange everything inside. This was the second kind—the breakup that didn't just end a relationship, it ended a version of yourself. The one that made you different after. Maybe it was your first real love, or the person you thought you'd marry, or someone who hurt you so badly you didn't recognize yourself in the aftermath. Either way, losing them changed you in ways you didn't see coming.

The heartbreak itself might have been sudden or slow. Maybe they ended it out of nowhere and you were blindsided. Maybe you saw it coming for months but couldn't stop it. Maybe it was mutual and necessary but still devastating. Maybe they cheated, or lied, or just stopped loving you and didn't know how to say it. Or maybe you were the one who had to walk away from something that was killing you even though you still loved them.

What happened after the breakup is the real story. The crying, the anger, the nights you couldn't sleep, the friends who held you together when you fell apart. The moments you thought you'd never recover. The slow, painful process of rebuilding yourself into someone who could function without them. Maybe you did things you're not proud of—called too many times, drove by their house, checked their social media obsessively. Maybe you handled it with dignity. Probably both.

That heartbreak taught you something you couldn't have learned any other way. About your own strength, about what you'd tolerate and what you wouldn't, about how to survive something that felt unsurvivable. You came out different on the other side—harder in some ways, softer in others, but undeniably changed.

Writing Prompt Questions

1. Who broke your heart, and how did it happen? Was it sudden or did you see it coming? What was the moment you knew it was over?

2. What made this heartbreak different from others? Why did this one crack you open in a way nothing else had? What made them so important?

3. What did you do in the first 24-48 hours after it ended? Did you fall apart, get angry, go numb? Describe those immediate first moments and hours.

4. In the weeks and months that followed, what was your lowest point? The night you thought you'd never get over it, the thing you did that you're not proud of, or the moment you scared yourself?

5. How did you eventually move forward? Was there a turning point, or did healing just happen gradually? Who or what helped you get through it?

6. How did that heartbreak change you? What do you know now about love, yourself, or relationships that you didn't know before? Are you grateful for what it taught you, or do you still carry the wound?

Your First Real Kiss

"A kiss is a secret told to the mouth instead of the ear."
— Ingrid Bergman

There are kisses, and then there's the first real one—the one that wasn't a dare or a peck at a middle school dance. The kiss that made your knees weak, your stomach flip, and your brain go completely blank. The one where you finally understood what all the songs and movies were about. It wasn't just lips touching—it was the moment everything before felt like practice and everything after felt different.

Maybe it happened in a car after a date, or behind the bleachers, or on someone's front porch when you were supposed to be saying goodnight. Maybe you'd been building toward it for weeks, or maybe it happened suddenly when neither of you planned it. Maybe you knew it was coming and spent the whole night wondering when, or maybe it caught you completely off guard and you had half a second to decide whether to pull away or lean in.

The details are what make it memorable. Who initiated it? Was it confident or fumbling? Did you know what you were doing, or were you figuring it out as you went? What did it feel like in the seconds after—exhilarating, terrifying, awkward, perfect? Did you replay it in your mind for days, or did you immediately want to do it again?

That first real kiss wasn't just about the person you were kissing. It was about discovering a version of yourself you didn't know existed—bolder, more alive, more aware of your own body and desires. That kiss changed something. It proved you weren't a kid anymore. It opened a door to a whole new world of possibility, intimacy, and connection. This is the story of the moment everything shifted.

Writing Prompt Questions

1. Who was it, and where did it happen? Set the scene: the location, the time of day or night, what led up to that moment. How old were you?

2. How did it start—who made the first move? Was it planned, or did it just happen? What was the moment right before when you both knew it was about to?

3. What do you remember about the actual kiss? Was it perfect, awkward, too much teeth, surprisingly good? How long did it last, and what were you thinking (if you were thinking at all)?

4. What happened immediately after? Did you say anything, or was there just silence? Did you kiss again, or was once enough for that moment? How did you leave things?

5. Did anyone know about it, or was it a secret? If you told someone, who was the first person you called or told? What did you say about it?

6. How did that kiss change things between you and that person? Did it lead somewhere, or was it just a moment? Looking back now, what does that kiss represent about who you were becoming?

The One That Got Away

"Of all sad words of tongue or pen, the saddest are these: 'It might have been.'"
— John Greenleaf Whittier

There's the person you married, the people you dated, and then there's the one that got away. The person you think about when you hear a certain song, or when you're stuck in traffic, or when you wonder how your life would have turned out if you'd made different choices. Maybe you were together and it ended badly. Maybe the timing was wrong. Maybe you never actually got together at all, and that's exactly why you still wonder.

What makes someone "the one that got away" isn't always rational. Maybe they weren't even right for you. Maybe the relationship would have been a disaster if you'd actually pursued it. But in your memory, they exist in this suspended state of possibility—what could have been, what might have happened, what you'll never know for sure. They're frozen in time as potential rather than reality, and that's part of what makes them so hard to let go of.

The story might be about bad timing—you met when one of you was unavailable, or moving away, or not ready. Or maybe it's about missed signals and misunderstood intentions. Maybe you were young and stupid and let fear make your decisions. Maybe you chose the safe path instead of the risky one, or someone else instead of them, and you've spent years wondering if you chose wrong. Or maybe they were the one who got away because they chose someone else, and you never got the chance to find out what you could have been.

Years later, you might still think about them. Not obsessively, not destructively, but occasionally. You wonder where they are, who they became, whether they ever think about you too. The one that got away stays with you precisely because the story never got its ending.

Writing Prompt Questions

1. Who were they, and how did you meet? What made them different from other people you dated or were interested in? What drew you to them?

2. What happened—or didn't happen—between you? Were you together briefly, almost together, or never officially together at all? Tell the story of what was or what might have been.

3. Why did it end, or why did it never start? Was it timing, circumstances, fear, someone else? What prevented this from becoming what it could have been?

4. Was there a specific moment when you knew they were slipping away? A conversation, a goodbye, a choice one of you made? What happened?

5. Have you ever reconnected or seen them again? If yes, what was that like? If no, have you been tempted to reach out, or do you prefer leaving it as a memory?

6. Looking back, do you think they really were "the one that got away," or is the fantasy better than the reality would have been? What does that person represent to you now?

The Worst Date Ever

"I've been on so many blind dates, I should get a free dog."
— Wendy Liebman

Most bad dates are just forgettable—boring conversation, no chemistry, you go home early and never think about them again. But then there's the worst date ever, the one so spectacularly bad it becomes a story you tell for decades. The date where everything that could go wrong did, or where the person revealed themselves to be so awful you couldn't believe you'd agreed to go out with them in the first place.

Maybe it started bad from the jump—they showed up late, looked nothing like their photo, or were rude to the waiter within the first five minutes. Maybe the conversation was painful, full of awkward silences or red flags you couldn't ignore. Or maybe it started fine and then took a turn—they got drunk, said something unforgivable, their ex showed up, or some disaster struck that turned the evening into a nightmare you couldn't escape.

The worst part about a truly terrible date is that you're stuck. You can't just leave without being rude, or you're too far from home, or you're trying to give them the benefit of the doubt even though every instinct is screaming at you to run. So you sit there, enduring it, watching the clock, planning your exit strategy while they're oblivious to how badly this is going. Maybe you excused yourself to the bathroom three times just to get a break. Maybe you texted a friend for a rescue call that never came.

Sometimes the worst dates are funny in hindsight—the absurdity of it, the sheer awfulness, the fact that you survived and have a great story. Other times they're just cringe-inducing memories you wish you could forget. Either way, that date taught you exactly what you didn't want, and possibly made you appreciate every decent date that came after. This is the story of the date that set the bar for "never again."

Writing Prompt Questions

1. Who were you on this date with, and how did it get set up? Was it a blind date, someone you met online, a friend of a friend? What were you expecting versus what you got?

2. What made it so terrible? Was it one big disaster or a series of smaller nightmares? Walk us through what went wrong and when you realized this was going to be bad.

3. What's the moment that made you think "I need to get out of here"? What was said or done that crossed the line from bad to unbearable?

4. How did you handle it? Did you tough it out until the end, fake an emergency and leave, or tell them directly this wasn't working? What was your exit strategy?

5. What happened after the date ended? Did they try to contact you again? Did you ghost them or tell them the truth? How did you escape permanently?

6. Looking back, is it funny now, or does it still make you cringe? What did that terrible date teach you about what to look for—or avoid—in future relationships?

Meeting Your In-Laws

"You can choose your friends, but you can't choose your family."
— Harper Lee

Meeting your partner's parents for the first time is a performance unlike any other. You're trying to be charming, polite, impressive—the person they'll feel good about their child bringing home. But you're also nervous as hell because you know this matters. Their opinion counts, even if you wish it didn't. And no matter how much your partner prepped you or tried to make it easier, walking into that house or restaurant knowing you were being evaluated changed everything.

Maybe it went well. Maybe they loved you immediately, welcomed you warmly, made you feel like you already belonged. Or maybe it was awkward—stilted conversation, uncomfortable silences, the sense that they were sizing you up and finding you lacking. Maybe they asked invasive questions about your job, your family, your intentions. Maybe they told embarrassing stories about your partner that revealed more than anyone wanted. Maybe the mom was cold, the dad was intimidating, or both of them made it clear you weren't what they had in mind.

The worst part was trying to read the room while being yourself, or at least a version of yourself that seemed acceptable. You monitored everything—how you dressed, what you said, how much you ate, whether you laughed at their jokes. You were hyperaware of every signal, every glance between the parents, every moment your partner seemed uncomfortable or proud or embarrassed. The whole experience felt like a test you hadn't studied for.

That first meeting set the tone for everything that came after. Maybe it got easier over time, or maybe it stayed awkward for years. Maybe you eventually won them over, or maybe you accepted that you'd never be exactly what they wanted. Either way, meeting the in-laws was a milestone—proof that this relationship was serious enough to involve families, ready or not.

Writing Prompt Questions

1. When and where did you meet your in-laws for the first time? What was the setup—dinner at their house, a restaurant, a holiday? How long had you been dating when this happened?

2. How did you prepare, and what were you most nervous about? Did your partner give you a rundown on what to expect, or did you go in blind?

3. What was the first impression like? How did they greet you, and what was the vibe in those first few minutes? Did they seem welcoming, skeptical, or something else?

4. What's the moment from that meeting that stands out most? Something awkward that was said, a question they asked, a look they gave, or a story they told?

5. How did your partner handle it? Were they supportive, embarrassed, apologetic? Did they defend you if needed, or leave you to fend for yourself?

6. Looking back, how did that first meeting shape your relationship with your in-laws? Did it get better over time, stay complicated, or was it always fine? What do you wish you'd known then?

Long Distance Love

"Absence sharpens love, presence strengthens it."
— Benjamin Franklin

Distance is supposed to kill relationships. Everyone says so. But sometimes distance does something else entirely—it reveals whether what you have is strong enough to survive airports, time zones, and months of missing someone so badly it physically hurts. Maybe it was college in different states, a military deployment, a job that took one of you far away, or just circumstances that put hundreds or thousands of miles between you when all you wanted was to be in the same room.

Long distance relationships require a different kind of commitment. You couldn't just show up at their door when you had a bad day. You couldn't hold their hand or fall asleep next to them. Every conversation was scheduled, every visit planned and counted down to like a holiday. Phone bills became astronomical. You learned each other's schedules by heart so you'd know when to call. You sent letters, emails, care packages—anything to bridge the gap between here and there.

The hardest part wasn't the distance itself—it was the life happening around you that they weren't part of. Friends asked why you didn't just date someone local. You watched other couples do normal couple things while you were in your room on the phone, again, trying to feel close to someone who was too far away to touch. Maybe you questioned whether it was worth it. Maybe you had moments when you wanted to quit because missing them was exhausting and you were tired of waiting.

That long distance relationship taught you whether love could survive on faith and phone calls. Maybe it did, and you're still together. Maybe it didn't, and the distance eventually won. Either way, you learned what you were capable of enduring for someone you loved.

Writing Prompt Questions

1. How did the distance happen—was it expected or did circumstances force you apart? Where were you, where were they, and how far apart were you?

2. How did you stay connected? Phone calls, letters, emails, video chats? What were your routines, and what time of day did you most look forward to talking?

3. What was the hardest part about being long distance? Was it the loneliness, watching other couples, the financial cost, or just missing them constantly? What almost broke you?

4. Describe the best reunion you had. What was it like seeing them again after weeks or months apart? Where did you meet, and what was that moment like?

5. Did anyone question why you were doing it? What did people say, and how did you defend your choice to stay together despite the distance?

6. How did the relationship end—did you finally close the distance, or did distance win? Looking back, was the long distance relationship worth what it cost you? What did it teach you about love and commitment?

Identity & Transformation

9 Memory Sparks

Finding or Losing Religion

"To thine own self be true."
— William Shakespeare

Religion shapes everything—how you see the world, what you believe about right and wrong, who you think you're supposed to be. And then something shifts. Maybe you found faith when you didn't have it before, or maybe you lost it after years of believing. Either way, your relationship with religion changed in a way that redefined your entire worldview, and there's no going back to how you saw things before.

If you found religion, you remember what led you there. Maybe it was a crisis that brought you to your knees, or a moment of clarity that felt like divine intervention, or a community that welcomed you when you needed belonging. Maybe you'd been searching for meaning and finally found it, or maybe faith found you when you weren't even looking. That awakening changed how you lived, what you valued, and who you became.

If you abandoned religion, you remember what broke. Maybe it was hypocrisy you couldn't ignore anymore, or rules that didn't make sense, or trauma inflicted in the name of faith. Maybe you asked questions no one could answer, or you realized you'd been performing belief without actually feeling it. Maybe you walked away angry, or sad, or relieved. Maybe it was gradual—a slow drift until one day you realized you didn't believe anymore. Or maybe it was sudden, a moment when everything you'd been taught crumbled and you had to rebuild from scratch.

Either way, changing your relationship with religion wasn't just a personal decision—it affected your family, your community, your identity. Some people understood. Others didn't. But you had to follow what felt true, even when it cost you something. This is the story of the moment your faith changed, and what you became after.

Writing Prompt Questions

1. What changed—did you find religion or walk away from it? What was your relationship with faith before this shift, and what prompted the change?

2. Was there a specific moment or event that triggered this awakening or abandonment? A crisis, a realization, a conversation, something you witnessed? What happened?

3. How did this change affect your daily life, your choices, or your sense of identity? What did you start or stop doing because of this shift in belief?

4. How did your family and community react? Did they support you, reject you, or try to change your mind? What was that like?

5. Was this change gradual or sudden? Did you wrestle with it for years, or did something click and you knew immediately? Walk us through that process.

6. Looking back, do you see this as a loss, a liberation, or something more complicated? What did finding or losing faith teach you about yourself and what you truly believe?

Rock Bottom

"Sometimes you have to hit rock bottom to realize which way is up."
— Unknown

Rock bottom doesn't announce itself. You don't wake up one morning and think "this is it, the lowest I'll ever be." It's usually quieter than that—a moment when you realize you've been falling for a while and you've finally stopped. Maybe you're broke, broken, addicted, lost, or so far from who you thought you'd be that you don't recognize yourself anymore. Rock bottom is the place where denial stops working and you have to face exactly how bad things have gotten.

What brings someone to rock bottom varies. Maybe it was addiction—drugs, alcohol, something else that took over your life until nothing else mattered. Maybe it was a catastrophic loss—a death, a divorce, a betrayal that shattered everything. Maybe it was mental health spiraling out of control, or financial ruin, or choices that compounded until you were buried under the consequences. Maybe it was all of it at once, a perfect storm of everything going wrong until there was nowhere left to fall.

Rock bottom feels like the end, but it's also weirdly clarifying. When you've lost everything, or come close enough to taste it, the bullshit falls away. You see yourself clearly, maybe for the first time. You see what led you here—the choices, the patterns, the denial, the pain you've been running from. And you have a choice: stay here, or start climbing out.

The story of rock bottom isn't just about how you got there—it's about what you did next. Did you ask for help, or did you try to save yourself? Who showed up when you needed them, and who disappeared? What was the first step back up, and how long did it take before you could breathe again? Rock bottom is the place where everything changes, if you let it.

Writing Prompt Questions

1. What was your rock bottom? Describe where you were in your life —financially, emotionally, mentally, physically. What had brought you to that point?

2. When did you realize you'd hit rock bottom? Was there a specific moment of clarity, or did it dawn on you gradually? What made you finally acknowledge how bad things had gotten?

3. What did rock bottom feel like? Describe the emotions, the physical sensations, the thoughts that went through your head. What was the worst part?

4. Who knew how bad things were, and who didn't? Did you hide it from people, or was it obvious? Who showed up for you, and who disappeared when you needed them most?

5. What was the turning point—the moment you decided to climb out? Was there something specific that made you choose to change, or did survival instinct just kick in?

6. How did you start rebuilding from rock bottom? What were the first steps, and how long did it take before you felt like yourself again? What did hitting bottom teach you that nothing else could have?

The Mentor

"When the student is ready, the teacher appears."
— Buddhist Proverb

Most people who shape your life do it quietly, over time, without fanfare or recognition. A mentor isn't always someone official—a teacher, a boss, a coach. Sometimes it's just someone who saw something in you that you didn't see in yourself, and took the time to draw it out. They believed in you when you didn't believe in yourself. They pushed you when you needed pushing, and caught you when you stumbled. They changed the trajectory of your life simply by paying attention.

Maybe you met them at work, or school, or in some unexpected place where you weren't looking for guidance but found it anyway. Maybe they were older and wiser, or maybe they were just someone who'd been where you were and knew the way through. What made them a mentor wasn't their credentials—it was their willingness to invest in you without expecting anything in return. They gave you their time, their wisdom, their honesty, and sometimes their tough love when you needed to hear hard truths.

The lessons they taught weren't always explicit. Sometimes it was watching how they handled a crisis, or how they treated people, or how they made decisions. Sometimes it was a conversation that lasted five minutes but stuck with you for decades. Sometimes it was just their presence—proof that someone like you could succeed, could survive, could become something more than what circumstances suggested.

That mentor changed your life in ways you might not have recognized at the time. They opened doors, shifted your perspective, gave you permission to want more or be more. Maybe you stayed in touch, or maybe life pulled you apart and you never properly thanked them. Either way, they left a mark. This is the story of the person who saw you, believed in you, and changed everything.

Writing Prompt Questions

1. Who was your mentor, and how did you meet them? What was the context—work, school, a chance encounter? How did the relationship begin?

2. What did they see in you that you didn't see in yourself? What quality, talent, or potential did they recognize before you did?

3. What's the most important lesson or piece of advice they gave you? Was it something they said directly, or something you learned by watching them?

4. Was there a specific moment when their guidance changed your trajectory? A conversation, an opportunity they created, a decision they helped you make?

5. Are they still in your life, or did you lose touch? If you lost touch, do you wish you could tell them something now? If they're still around, have you thanked them?

6. How did that mentorship change who you became? What would be different about your life if you'd never met them? What do you hope to pass on from what they taught you?

The Diagnosis

"Life is not the way it's supposed to be. It's the way it is."
— Virginia Satir

There's before the diagnosis, and there's after. The moment a doctor tells you something is wrong with your body—something serious, something that changes everything—creates a dividing line in your life. Maybe you suspected something was off and the diagnosis confirmed your fears. Or maybe it blindsided you completely, turning an ordinary day into the day everything changed. Either way, hearing those words out loud made it real in a way it wasn't before.

The diagnosis itself might have been delivered clinically, matter-of-factly, or with compassion. Maybe the doctor gave you statistics and treatment options and tried to sound hopeful. Maybe they were blunt and gave it to you straight. Maybe you cried right there in the office, or maybe you went numb and didn't process it until later when you were alone. The words themselves—the medical terminology, the prognosis, the implications—landed like a bomb, and the aftermath was figuring out how to keep living with this new information.

What came after the diagnosis is the real story. The decisions you had to make about treatment, the people you had to tell, the fear you had to manage while pretending to be strong. Maybe you fought it with everything you had. Maybe you had to learn to live with it as a chronic condition. Maybe it changed your body, your capabilities, your entire sense of who you were. Maybe you survived it and came out different on the other side.

A diagnosis forces you to reckon with mortality, vulnerability, and the fragility of the body you've been living in without thinking about it. It strips away the illusion of control and makes you face what's real. This is the story of the moment you found out, and what you became in the aftermath of knowing.

Writing Prompt Questions

1. What was the diagnosis, and how did you find out? Were you expecting bad news, or did it come out of nowhere? Describe the moment the doctor told you.

2. What was your immediate reaction? Did you cry, go numb, ask questions, or just sit there trying to process? What went through your mind in those first moments?

3. Who did you tell first, and what was that conversation like? How did you find the words to say it out loud, and how did they react?

4. What decisions did you have to make after the diagnosis? Treatment options, lifestyle changes, how to move forward? Walk us through what came next.

5. How did the diagnosis change your life—your body, your routine, your sense of self? What had to change, and what stayed the same?

6. Looking back, how has living with this diagnosis shaped who you are? What did it teach you about strength, vulnerability, or what really matters? Are you grateful for anything that came from it, or is it just something you've survived?

The Name You'd Choose

"I define me. Nobody else."
— Mary J. Blige

You've been answering to the same name your whole life, but there's probably been a moment—maybe many moments—when you heard a different name and thought "That should have been mine." Maybe it was a character in a book, someone you met who carried their name like it was made for them, or just a name you've always loved for reasons you can't explain. That name lives in your head as an alternate version of yourself, the one who got to choose.

Some people love their names. They fit perfectly, like they were custom-made. But for others, your name has always felt like wearing someone else's clothes—technically functional, but never quite right. Maybe it's too soft when you're sharp-edged, too old-fashioned when you're forward-thinking, or too conventional when everything about you rebels against convention. Maybe it was chosen by people who didn't know you yet and couldn't have predicted who you'd become.

The name you'd choose for yourself says everything about the gap between who you were supposed to be and who you actually are. Maybe you'd pick something bold that commands attention, or something understated that lets you move through the world on your own terms. Maybe you'd reclaim a name from your heritage that got anglicized, or choose something that has nothing to do with where you came from. Maybe you just want a name that feels like yours instead of theirs.

If you could introduce yourself tomorrow with any name you wanted, what would it be? And what does that name tell you about the woman you've become versus the girl they named all those years ago?

Writing Prompt Questions

1. Do you like your given name, or have you always wished it were different? What's your relationship with the name you were given, and why?

2. If you could rename yourself, what name would you choose? Why that specific name—what does it represent or feel like to you?

3. Who were you named after, or why did your parents choose your name? Does knowing the story behind it make you like it more or less?

4. Have you ever gone by a nickname, a middle name, or a different name entirely? How did that come about, and did it fit better than your given name?

5. If you've legally changed your name or seriously considered it, what prompted that? What did it take to finally make that choice?

6. What does your ideal name say about who you are versus who people expected you to be? How would your life feel different if you'd always been called that name?

Not Caring What People Think

"Be yourself; everyone else is already taken."
— Oscar Wilde

For most of your life, you probably cared what people thought. You dressed a certain way, said the right things, tried to fit in or at least not stand out too much. You edited yourself constantly, second-guessed your choices, and shaped your life around avoiding judgment. Their opinions mattered. Their approval felt necessary. And then one day, something shifted. Maybe it was gradual, or maybe it happened all at once, but suddenly you just didn't care anymore.

Maybe it was triggered by something specific—a moment when someone judged you anyway despite all your efforts to be acceptable, or a realization that the people whose opinions you valued most didn't actually know you at all. Maybe you just got tired. Tired of performing, tired of shrinking, tired of living for an audience that would never be satisfied no matter what you did. Whatever caused it, something broke loose, and you decided you were done.

The freedom that came after was disorienting at first. Without the constant background noise of "what will they think," you had to figure out what you actually wanted. What you actually believed. Who you actually were when no one was watching or evaluating. Some people didn't like the version of you that emerged. That was the point—you weren't asking for their approval anymore.

This wasn't about becoming reckless or cruel. It was about becoming honest. It was about choosing authenticity over acceptance, your own voice over their comfort. The moment you stopped caring what people thought was the moment you started living as yourself. Some relationships couldn't survive that shift. Others got stronger because they were finally built on truth instead of performance. Either way, you were free.

Writing Prompt Questions

1. When did you realize you'd stopped caring what people thought? Was there a specific moment, or did it dawn on you gradually? What were you doing when you noticed the shift?

2. What triggered it—did something happen that made you stop caring, or did you just wake up one day and decide you were done? Describe the catalyst or the buildup that led to your liberation.

3. What's the first thing you did differently once you stopped caring? How did you dress, speak, or show up in the world once their opinions no longer mattered?

4. Who noticed the change, and how did they react? Did anyone try to pull you back into line? Did some people disappear from your life because you weren't playing the game anymore?

5. What did it feel like to finally stop performing for an audience? Was it terrifying, exhilarating, lonely, freeing? Did you miss the approval, or was letting it go easier than you expected?

6. What advice would you give someone still trapped in worrying about what people think? What do you know now that you wish you'd understood sooner?

Near-Death Experience

"Life is what happens when you're busy making other plans."
— John Lennon

Most people go through life assuming they have time—time to fix things, time to take risks, time to become who they want to be. And then something happens that brings you face-to-face with your own mortality, and suddenly time feels like the most precious thing you've ever had. Maybe it was an accident, a health crisis, violence, or just being in the wrong place at the wrong moment. Whatever it was, you came close enough to death to feel it, and that changes everything.

The moment itself is usually chaos—adrenaline, fear, your brain moving too fast or shutting down completely. Maybe you saw it coming and had seconds to prepare, or maybe it happened so fast you didn't have time to be afraid. Maybe you fought to survive, or maybe survival was out of your hands and all you could do was wait to see if you'd make it. Time warps in those moments. Seconds feel like hours. Or everything happens so fast you can't piece it together until later.

What comes after is the real transformation. You survived, but you're not the same person who almost died. Maybe you're grateful for every ordinary day in a way you never were before. Maybe you're angry at how fragile everything is. Maybe you're reckless now, or more cautious, or both depending on the moment. Maybe you see people differently—the ones who showed up, the ones who didn't, the ones who understood and the ones who moved on like it didn't happen.

A near-death experience strips away illusions. It forces you to confront what actually matters, what you've been wasting time on, and what you'd regret if you ran out of chances. This is the story of the moment you almost didn't make it, and who you became after.

Writing Prompt Questions

1. What happened that brought you close to death? Set the scene—where were you, what was happening, and when did you realize you might not survive?

2. What went through your mind in that moment? Were you scared, calm, thinking clearly, or did your brain shut down? What do you remember feeling or thinking?

3. How did you survive? Was it luck, someone's intervention, your own actions, or a combination? Walk us through what saved you.

4. What happened immediately after—in the hours or days following? What was it like processing that you'd almost died? Who did you tell, and how did they react?

5. How did that experience change you? Did you become more grateful, more reckless, more careful? Did your priorities shift? What did you start or stop doing because of it?

6. Looking back, what did that near-death experience teach you about life, yourself, or what really matters? Do you think about it often, or have you made peace with it and moved on?

Biggest Physical Transformation

"Take care of your body. It's the only place you have to live."
— Jim Rohn

Your body tells a story, and sometimes that story involves a dramatic transformation. Maybe you lost a significant amount of weight, or gained it. Maybe you got strong after years of feeling weak, or recovered from an injury that changed how you moved through the world. Maybe you went through pregnancy and your body was never the same after. Maybe you changed your appearance so drastically that people didn't recognize you. Whatever it was, your physical transformation wasn't just about how you looked—it was about who you became in the process.

The decision to transform usually comes from somewhere deep. Maybe you were tired of feeling uncomfortable in your own skin, or a health scare forced you to change, or you just decided one day that you were done settling for a body that didn't feel like yours. Maybe it was about reclaiming control, or proving something to yourself, or becoming the physical version of who you already were inside. The motivation mattered, because transformation is hard and you needed a reason strong enough to keep going when it got difficult.

The process itself was probably harder than you expected. The discipline required, the setbacks, the moments you wanted to quit. Maybe people commented on your changing body in ways that felt invasive or judgmental. Maybe they supported you, or maybe they felt threatened by your transformation and tried to sabotage it. Maybe you did it alone, or maybe you had help. Either way, you had to show up for yourself every single day and choose the harder path.

When you finally achieved the transformation, it wasn't just physical. You proved to yourself that you were capable of change, that you could commit to something difficult and see it through. Your body became evidence of your willpower, your resilience, your refusal to stay stuck.

Writing Prompt Questions

1. What was your biggest physical transformation? Weight loss, muscle gain, recovery from injury, pregnancy, surgery, a complete style change? Describe what changed and how dramatic it was.

2. What motivated you to transform? Was it health, vanity, proving something, reclaiming yourself? What finally pushed you to commit to the change?

3. What was the hardest part of the transformation process? The discipline, the sacrifices, the setbacks? What almost made you quit, and what kept you going?

4. How did people react to your transformation? Did they support you, get jealous, make comments? How did their reactions affect you?

5. How did transforming your body change how you felt about yourself? Did it give you confidence, peace, strength? What shifted internally when your exterior changed?

6. Looking back, was the transformation worth it? Do you still maintain it, or did things shift again? What did that physical change teach you about yourself and what you're capable of?

Losing Your Virginity

"Vulnerability is the birthplace of love, belonging, joy, courage, empathy, and creativity." — Brené Brown

Everyone has a story about their first time, and very few of them are the romantic, perfect moment you imagined when you were younger. Maybe yours was planned—you'd been with someone for a while, felt ready, and chose the moment deliberately. Or maybe it was spontaneous, awkward, or happened under circumstances you didn't expect. Maybe it was with someone you loved, or someone you thought you loved, or someone you barely knew. Whatever the details, that experience marked a before and after in your life.

The decision to have sex for the first time carries weight. Maybe you felt ready and empowered, or maybe you felt pressured—by them, by your friends, by the idea that everyone else was already doing it. Maybe you were curious, or in love, or just tired of being the virgin. Maybe you'd thought about it for months, or maybe it happened faster than you planned and you went with it. Either way, once it happened, you couldn't take it back, and you had to figure out how you felt about that.

What you remember most might not be the act itself—it might be the moment after, lying there processing what just happened. Or the conversation before, trying to navigate consent and expectations. Or the aftermath—how you felt the next day, whether things changed between you and that person, whether you told anyone or kept it secret. Maybe you felt proud, or disappointed, or just relieved it was over. Maybe it hurt more than you expected, or felt more emotional, or was more anticlimactic than years of buildup suggested it would be.

Losing your virginity is one of those experiences everyone remembers differently. For some, it's meaningful and empowering. For others, it's complicated or regrettable. Either way, it changed how you saw yourself, your body, and intimacy. This is the story of your first time, unfiltered.

Writing Prompt Questions

1. Who was it with, and what was your relationship? Were you dating, in love, friends, or something else? How old were you, and how long had you known them?

2. Was it planned or spontaneous? Had you talked about it ahead of time, or did it just happen? What led up to that moment?

3. How did you feel about it in the moment and immediately after? Emotional, empowered, disappointed, relieved? What was going through your mind?

4. Did you tell anyone afterward? Who was the first person you told, if anyone, and what did you say? Or did you keep it private?

5. How did losing your virginity change things between you and that person? Did the relationship continue, end, or just shift into something different?

6. Looking back now, how do you feel about that experience? Do you wish it had been different, or are you at peace with how it happened? What did that first time teach you about yourself, intimacy, or what you needed?

Motherhood

9 Memory Sparks

Becoming a Mother

"A mother's love is whole no matter how many times divided."
— Robert Brault

Becoming a mother is supposed to be this transcendent, beautiful moment where everything makes sense and love floods through you like a tidal wave. And maybe that happened for you. Or maybe it was messier than that—terrifying, overwhelming, confusing, and nothing like what the books promised. Maybe you felt love immediately, or maybe it took days or weeks for that feeling to show up. Maybe you were ready, or maybe you looked at this tiny human and thought "I have no idea what I'm doing." Both versions are true. Both versions are allowed.

The day you became a mother—whether through birth, adoption, or stepping into that role in some other way—changed everything. Your body, your identity, your priorities, your sleep schedule, your entire sense of self. You crossed a line that day, and there was no going back to who you were before. Some parts of that were beautiful. Some parts were brutal. Nobody tells you how lonely it can feel even when you're never alone, or how hard it is to lose yourself while simultaneously finding a new version of yourself you didn't know existed.

Maybe you had support, or maybe you were figuring it out on your own. Maybe your partner was helpful, or maybe they had no clue either. Maybe your own mother showed up, or maybe her advice made everything worse. Maybe you felt like you were drowning, or maybe you took to it naturally, or maybe it was both depending on the hour.

This is the real story of that day—not the version you told everyone, but the one you lived. The beautiful parts, the hard parts, the parts that surprised you.

Writing Prompt Questions

1. Describe the actual moment you became a mother—what do you remember about that day? Not the sanitized version, but the real one. What did it feel like physically, emotionally, mentally?

2. What did you feel when you first held your child (or first knew you were their mother)? Was it instant love, or something more complicated? Be honest about what you actually felt, not what you thought you were supposed to feel.

3. What was the hardest part of those first days or weeks? The exhaustion, the fear, the physical recovery, the total loss of control? What did you struggle with that nobody warned you about?

4. What surprised you most about becoming a mother? Something you didn't expect to feel, do, or experience? What caught you completely off guard?

5. Was there a moment in those early days when you doubted yourself or wondered if you'd made a mistake? What were you thinking, and how did you get through it?

6. What do you wish you could tell your children about what it was really like when they were born? What do you want them to understand about that time that they don't know?

The Lie You Told Your Kids

"The truth will set you free, but first it will piss you off."
— Gloria Steinem

Every parent lies to their kids. Some lies are harmless—Santa Claus, the Tooth Fairy, "the ice cream truck only plays music when it's out of ice cream." But then there are the other lies, the ones that mattered more. Maybe you lied to protect them from something they were too young to understand. Maybe you lied to protect yourself from questions you weren't ready to answer. Maybe you lied because the truth was too complicated, too painful, or just too damn hard to explain to a child.

The lie might have been about their father, or your past, or why you had to move, or where the money went, or why you were crying in the bathroom. Maybe you told them everything was fine when it absolutely wasn't. Maybe you said you and their dad still loved each other when the marriage was already over. Maybe you pretended to be stronger, happier, or more together than you actually were because they needed you to be, and you couldn't let them see you fall apart.

Some lies were strategic—told to spare them from adult problems they shouldn't have to carry. Others were survival—told because you were barely holding it together and the truth would have broken something you couldn't afford to break. Either way, you carried that lie, knowing eventually they might find out, knowing you might have to answer for it someday.

Maybe they never found out. Maybe they discovered the truth years later and confronted you, or maybe they figured it out on their own and never said anything. Maybe the lie protected them, or maybe it created distance you never fully closed. Either way, you did what you thought was right at the time, with the information and resources you had.

Writing Prompt Questions

1. What did you lie to your kids about? Was it something small or something significant? What was the lie, and why did you tell it?

2. How old were they when you told the lie, and what prompted it? Was it a question they asked, a situation that forced your hand, or something you chose to hide proactively?

3. What was the truth you were protecting them from (or protecting yourself from having to explain)? Why couldn't you tell them the real story at that time?

4. Did they ever find out the truth? If yes, how did they discover it, and what was their reaction? If no, do you think they suspect, or did the lie hold?

5. Do you regret the lie, or do you think it was the right call given the circumstances? Would you tell the truth if you could go back, or would you lie again?

6. What did that lie teach you about parenting, honesty, and the impossible choices you have to make to protect your kids—or yourself?

Mother's Intuition

"Mothers are all slightly insane."
— J.D. Salinger

There's knowing something logically, and then there's knowing something in your gut—that inexplicable certainty that something is wrong, or right, or about to happen. Mother's intuition isn't mystical, but it feels that way sometimes. Maybe you woke up in the middle of the night knowing your child needed you before they cried. Maybe you sensed danger before there was any logical reason to worry. Maybe you just knew something was off even when everyone else said you were overreacting.

The moment itself is hard to explain to people who haven't experienced it. There's no evidence, no proof, just this overwhelming sense that you need to act. Maybe it was about your child's health—you knew something was wrong before the doctors did, and you pushed until they took you seriously. Maybe it was about their safety—you felt uneasy about a person or situation and pulled them out of it just in time. Maybe it was smaller but just as real—you knew they were lying, or hurt, or in trouble, even when they swore everything was fine.

What makes mother's intuition powerful isn't just that you felt it—it's that you trusted it enough to act on it, even when it seemed irrational. Maybe people questioned you, told you that you were being paranoid or overprotective. Maybe you second-guessed yourself, wondered if you were losing your mind. But you listened to that voice anyway, and you were right.

That moment when your intuition saved the day, protected your child, or caught something everyone else missed—that's the story. It's proof that being a mother gives you a kind of knowledge that doesn't come from books or logic. It comes from somewhere deeper, and it's real even when you can't explain it.

Writing Prompt Questions

1. What did your intuition tell you? Describe the feeling—was it a sense of dread, a nagging worry, a sudden certainty? What were you picking up on that no one else saw?

2. What was happening at the time? Set the scene—where were you, what was your child doing, and what triggered that gut feeling?

3. How did you act on your intuition? Did you intervene immediately, investigate further, or push back against people who told you nothing was wrong? What did you do?

4. Were you right? What happened that confirmed your intuition was accurate? Did you prevent something, discover something, or catch something just in time?

5. Did anyone doubt you or try to talk you out of trusting your gut? How did you handle their skepticism, and what made you trust yourself anyway?

6. Looking back, what do you think that intuition was—instinct, pattern recognition, divine intervention, or something else? Do you trust your gut more now because of that experience?

Mom Guilt

"There is no way to be a perfect mother, but a million ways to be a good one."
— Unknown

Mom guilt is a special kind of torture that starts the moment you become a mother and never fully goes away. It's the voice that tells you you're doing everything wrong—working too much or not enough, being too strict or too lenient, giving too much attention or not enough. It's the weight of every choice you make, wondering if you're screwing up your kids in ways you won't understand until they're in therapy years from now.

Maybe your guilt is about something specific—the time you lost your temper and said something you can't take back, the event you missed because of work, the decision to stay in a bad marriage or leave a good one. Maybe it's about choosing yourself when you were supposed to be selfless, or being too tired to be present, or letting them watch too much TV because you needed ten minutes of peace. Maybe it's about the things you couldn't give them—the house you couldn't afford, the stability you couldn't provide, the childhood you wish they'd had.

The worst part about mom guilt is that it's impossible to win. No matter what you choose, there's a voice telling you that you chose wrong. You feel guilty for working and guilty for staying home. Guilty for being too involved and guilty for giving them independence. Guilty for enforcing rules and guilty for being too permissive. The guilt is relentless, and it's exhausting.

But here's what nobody tells you: your kids probably don't remember half the things you're beating yourself up over. They remember whether you showed up, whether you loved them, whether you tried. Perfect mothers don't exist, and your kids don't need one. They need you—flawed, human, doing your best with what you have.

Writing Prompt Questions

1. What's the thing you feel most guilty about as a mother? The choice you made, the moment you regret, the thing you wish you could go back and do differently?

2. When did that guilt start, and has it ever gone away? Is it something that haunts you constantly, or does it surface at specific times?

3. Have you ever talked to your kids about what you feel guilty for? If yes, what did they say? If no, what stops you from bringing it up?

4. Looking back rationally, was the thing you feel guilty about really as bad as you've made it out to be? Or have you been carrying unnecessary weight?

5. What would you say to another mother struggling with the same guilt you carry? Would you judge her as harshly as you judge yourself?

6. If you could let go of one piece of mom guilt, which would it be? What would it take for you to forgive yourself and move forward?

Catching Your Kid

"Your children will become what you are; so be what you want them to be."
— David Bly

You remember being caught as a kid—the moment someone walked in at exactly the wrong time and you had nowhere to hide. Now you're on the other side of it. You're the parent who walked in, looked up, or checked their phone at the exact moment that revealed what your child was really up to. Maybe you suspected something was off and went looking for proof. Or maybe you stumbled onto it completely by accident and wished you hadn't.

What you caught them doing matters less than the moment itself. Maybe it was sneaking out, drinking, smoking, lying about where they were, or something they swore they'd never do. Maybe it was bigger—stealing, drugs, something that scared you because you'd been there yourself and knew how badly it could go. Or maybe it was smaller but still significant—a relationship they were hiding, a secret they'd been keeping, a side of themselves they didn't want you to see.

The confrontation that followed is burned into your memory. What did you say? Were you angry, disappointed, calm, or did you lose it completely? Did you handle it the way you wanted to, or did you react in the moment and regret it later? Did they confess immediately, try to lie their way out of it, or shut down completely? And what happened after—punishment, conversation, or just a long, uncomfortable silence?

Catching your kid forces you to reckon with the fact that they're human, flawed, and capable of making the same mistakes you made. Maybe worse, maybe better, but definitely not perfect. It's the moment you realize you can't protect them from everything, including themselves. This is the story of what you caught them doing, and how both of you survived the aftermath.

Writing Prompt Questions

1. What did you catch your kid doing, and how did you find out? Did you go looking for evidence, or did you stumble onto it accidentally?

2. What was the moment you realized what was happening? Describe the scene—where were you, what did you see or find, and what went through your mind?

3. How did you confront them? What did you say, and how did they react? Did they confess, lie, cry, or shut down completely?

4. What emotions were you feeling—anger, disappointment, fear, or something else? Were you thinking about your own past and the mistakes you made at their age?

5. What consequences did you impose, if any? How did you handle it, and do you think you handled it well, or do you wish you'd done it differently?

6. Looking back, how did that moment change your relationship with your child? Did it create distance, build trust through honesty, or just become another chapter in the complicated story of raising them?

The Talk

"Speak the truth, even if your voice shakes."
— Maggie Kuhn

Every parent dreads "the talk"—that conversation you know you need to have but would rather avoid forever. Maybe it was the sex talk, or the drugs talk, or the "your father and I are getting divorced" talk. Maybe it was explaining death, or racism, or why bad things happen to good people. Whatever it was, you knew it was coming, you prepared as best you could, and then when the moment arrived, every carefully planned word flew out of your head.

The setup matters. Maybe you initiated it because you knew they were old enough and needed to hear it from you before they heard it from someone else. Or maybe they asked a question you couldn't dodge, and suddenly you were in the middle of a conversation you weren't ready for. Maybe you sat them down formally, or maybe it happened in the car where neither of you had to make eye contact. Either way, you were trying to explain something complicated to someone who might not be ready to understand it.

What you said—or tried to say—probably came out awkward. You stumbled over words, used metaphors that didn't quite land, or gave too much information and watched their face register regret for asking. Or maybe you gave too little and they walked away more confused than before. Maybe they asked questions you didn't know how to answer. Maybe they didn't ask anything at all, just sat there processing while you wondered what was going through their head.

The talk doesn't usually end the way you expect. Sometimes it goes better than you thought. Sometimes it's a disaster. But you had it, and that matters. This is the story of the conversation you didn't want to have but needed to.

Writing Prompt Questions

1. What was "the talk" you had to have with your kid? What topic were you dreading discussing, and what made it necessary to finally address it?

2. How did the conversation start? Did you plan it and sit them down, or did they ask a question that forced your hand? Set the scene—where were you?

3. What did you actually say? How did you explain it, and did it come out the way you intended, or was it awkward and fumbling?

4. How did they react? Were they embarrassed, curious, relieved, or upset? What questions did they ask, and how did you handle them?

5. Was there a moment during the talk when you realized you were saying too much, too little, or just the wrong thing? How did you recover?

6. Looking back, how do you think you did? Do you wish you'd handled it differently, or are you satisfied with how it went? Did it change your relationship with them?

Single Motherhood

"I can do hard things."
— Glennon Doyle

Being a single mother isn't a choice most women make—it's a reality you adapt to when circumstances change. Maybe the father left, or died, or was never really there to begin with. Maybe you left him because staying was worse than going it alone. Either way, you became the only parent in the room, responsible for everything—the money, the decisions, the discipline, the comfort, the future. There was no one to tag in when you were exhausted, no one to split the load, no backup plan.

The hardest part wasn't just doing everything yourself—it was the weight of knowing that if you failed, there was no safety net. Every decision felt heavier because you were the only one making it. Every bill felt more urgent because you were the only one paying it. Every bedtime, every meal, every school event, every crisis—all of it landed on you. And you showed up anyway, because what other choice did you have?

Single motherhood also meant judgment. People assumed things about you, about why you were alone, about whether you were doing it right. Some offered help. Others offered opinions you didn't ask for. You learned quickly who actually supported you and who just liked to talk. You also learned that you were stronger than you thought, more resourceful, more capable of surviving on less sleep and less money than seemed humanly possible.

Your kids might not have had everything, but they had you—fully present, fully committed, doing the work of two parents on your own. Maybe it made you closer to them, or maybe the stress created distance you're still trying to close. Either way, you did it. You raised them alone, and that takes a kind of strength most people never have to find.

Writing Prompt Questions

1. How did you become a single mother? What happened that left you parenting alone—divorce, death, abandonment, choice? Tell the story of when everything changed.

2. What was the hardest part of single motherhood for you? The financial pressure, the loneliness, the exhaustion, the weight of every decision? What nearly broke you?

3. Was there a moment when you realized you were actually going to survive this? A turning point when you stopped feeling like you were drowning and started feeling capable?

4. Who showed up for you during that time, and who disappeared? Were you surprised by who helped and who didn't? How did you handle doing it mostly alone?

5. How do you think being a single mother affected your relationship with your kids? Did it make you closer, or did the stress create challenges? Be honest about both the good and the hard.

6. Looking back, what do you want your kids to understand about what it took to raise them alone? What do you wish they knew about that time that they might not remember or realize?

The Tantrum in Public

"Insanity is hereditary; you get it from your children."
— Sam Levenson

Every parent has lived through the nightmare of a public meltdown. Your child losing their absolute mind in the middle of a store, restaurant, or some other place where everyone can see and judge. Maybe they were overtired, overstimulated, or just decided that this was the hill they were willing to die on. Either way, they went from zero to nuclear in seconds, and suddenly you were the star of a show you never auditioned for.

The tantrum itself was spectacular. Screaming, crying, throwing themselves on the floor, or going completely limp when you tried to pick them up. Maybe they wanted something you said no to, or maybe the trigger was something ridiculous like the wrong color cup or a sock that felt weird. It didn't matter what started it—once they were in it, there was no reasoning with them. They were a tiny tyrant, and you were just trying to survive.

What made it worse was the audience. The people staring, whispering, or offering unsolicited advice. The judgmental looks from strangers who clearly thought you were a terrible parent raising a terrible child. Maybe someone said something—"my kids never acted like that" or "a little discipline would fix that"—and you had to resist the urge to lose it yourself. Meanwhile, you're trying everything—bribing, threatening, ignoring, staying calm—and nothing is working.

Eventually it ended. Maybe they wore themselves out, or you physically removed them from the situation, or you gave in just to make it stop. You survived it, but you were exhausted and humiliated and questioning every parenting choice you'd ever made. This is the story of your child's most epic public meltdown, and how you lived to tell about it.

Writing Prompt Questions

1. Where were you when the tantrum happened, and what triggered it? Set the scene—what store, restaurant, or public place, and what set your child off?

2. How old was your child, and what did the meltdown look like? Describe the chaos—the screaming, the dramatics, the physical performance of their rage.

3. What did you try to do to stop it? Walk us through your attempts—bribing, reasoning, ignoring, threatening—and what (if anything) eventually worked.

4. How did people around you react? Did anyone help, judge, offer advice, or just stare? What was said or done that made it worse?

5. How did it finally end? Did they calm down on their own, did you remove them physically, or did you give in to their demands just to make it stop?

6. Looking back, can you laugh about it now, or does it still make you cringe? What did that experience teach you about parenting, public judgment, or your own limits?

The Pregnancy Test

"And suddenly you know: It's time to start something new and trust the magic of beginnings." — Meister Eckhart

There's a specific kind of waiting that happens in the three minutes between taking a pregnancy test and reading the results. Your entire life could change based on what that little stick says, and you're standing in a bathroom trying to breathe normally while your heart pounds so hard you can feel it everywhere. Maybe you were hoping for a positive result. Maybe you were praying for a negative. Maybe you had no idea what you wanted until you saw what you got.

The moment you decided to take the test tells its own story. Maybe your period was late and you knew, deep down, before you ever peed on that stick. Maybe you felt different—exhausted, nauseous, just off in a way you couldn't explain. Or maybe someone else suggested you take one and you laughed it off until you couldn't anymore. Maybe you bought the test weeks ago and it sat in your cabinet while you worked up the courage to use it, or maybe you grabbed it on impulse at the pharmacy and took it the second you got home.

What you felt when you saw the result—positive or negative—was probably complicated. Relief, panic, joy, devastation, or some confusing combination of all of them at once. Maybe you cried. Maybe you laughed. Maybe you just stood there staring at it, trying to absorb what it meant for your life, your body, your future, your relationship. Maybe you immediately knew what you'd do next, or maybe you had absolutely no idea.

That pregnancy test result changed something. Maybe it started the journey to becoming a mother, or maybe it didn't. Maybe it confirmed what you already knew, or maybe it shocked you completely. Either way, those few minutes in that bathroom were a turning point, and you'll never forget what you felt when you looked down and saw the answer.

Writing Prompt Questions

1. What made you decide to take the pregnancy test? Was your period late, were you feeling symptoms, or did someone suggest it? What was happening that made you think you might be pregnant?

2. Where were you when you took it, and were you alone? Describe the setting—your bathroom, a friend's house, a public restroom? Who knew you were taking it, if anyone?

3. What were you hoping for while you waited for the result? Did you want it to be positive or negative? Or were you genuinely unsure what you wanted?

4. What happened when you saw the result? What did it say, and what was your immediate reaction? What did you feel, say, or do in that first moment?

5. Who was the first person you told, and how did they react? Or did you keep it to yourself for a while? What was that conversation like?

6. How did that pregnancy test result change your life? Did it lead to becoming a mother, or to a different decision? Looking back, what does that moment represent about a turning point in your life?

Defiance & Standing up

9 Memory Sparks

The Confrontation

"The most courageous act is still to think for yourself. Aloud."
— Coco Chanel

Some arguments simmer for years before they finally explode. You bite your tongue, swallow your words, let things slide because confrontation feels worse than silence. But then something happens—a final comment, a last straw, a moment when you just can't hold it in anymore—and suddenly you're in the middle of a confrontation you've been avoiding for months or maybe years. Everything you've been holding back comes pouring out, and there's no taking it back.

The confrontation might have been with anyone—a partner, a parent, a friend, a boss, a family member who'd been overstepping for too long. Maybe it was calm and controlled, or maybe it was loud and messy. Maybe you planned what you were going to say, or maybe it erupted spontaneously and you said things you didn't know you were thinking until they were already out of your mouth. Either way, it was the moment you stopped swallowing your truth and made them hear it.

What you said mattered less than the fact that you finally said it. Maybe you called them out on their behavior, set a boundary they'd been crossing, or told them a truth they didn't want to hear. Maybe you were shaking, or crying, or so angry your voice was steady with rage. Maybe they fought back, or maybe they were shocked into silence. Maybe they apologized, or got defensive, or tried to make you the villain for finally speaking up.

The aftermath of a confrontation changes relationships. Some survived it and became stronger because honesty replaced pretense. Others didn't survive because the truth was too much to come back from. Either way, you proved to yourself that your voice mattered, even when using it was terrifying.

Writing Prompt Questions

1. Who did you confront, and what had they done that finally pushed you over the edge? What was the final straw after tolerating too much for too long?

2. What did you actually say? Can you remember the words you used? Was it planned, or did it come out in the heat of the moment? Did you say everything you wanted to say, or did you hold some back?

3. How did they react? Were they shocked, defensive, angry? Did they back down, or did it escalate? What happened in the moments immediately after you spoke up?

4. Was anyone else there to witness it? How did they react—did they support you, stay silent, or try to smooth things over? Did their response surprise you?

5. What did it feel like after you did it? Relief? Fear? Regret? Empowerment? How long did it take for your hands to stop shaking?

6. Did the confrontation change your relationship, or change you? Did things get better, worse, or just different? What did you learn about yourself from finally speaking up?

Setting Boundaries

"You get what you tolerate."
— Henry Cloud

For years, maybe you said yes when you meant no. You let people take more than you wanted to give. You accommodated, adjusted, made yourself smaller or more available because that's what was expected. You told yourself it was fine, that this is what good daughters or mothers or friends or employees do. Until one day, it wasn't fine anymore. Something shifted, and you finally drew a line. This far, no further. The boundary you should've set years ago but didn't have the courage or clarity to enforce until now.

Setting a boundary isn't easy, especially with people who've gotten used to you not having any. They don't always take it well when you suddenly change the rules. Maybe they called you selfish, acted hurt, or tried to guilt you into backing down. Maybe they tested the boundary immediately to see if you really meant it. Maybe some relationships couldn't survive your refusal to keep playing the old game.

The boundary might've been about time—saying no to obligations that drained you. Or emotional labor—refusing to manage everyone else's feelings anymore. Or physical space—deciding who gets access to you and when. Or money—stopping the financial drain of people who always needed something. Whatever it was, enforcing it required you to tolerate someone's disappointment, anger, or confusion. And you did it anyway.

That boundary changed things. Maybe it made some relationships better because they finally had honest limits. Maybe it ended relationships that only worked when you had no boundaries at all. Either way, you chose yourself. And that's not selfish—that's survival. This is the story of the line you drew, and what happened when you refused to erase it.

Writing Prompt Questions

1. What boundary did you finally set, and with whom? What were you no longer willing to tolerate, give, or do? What line did you draw?

2. What took you so long to set it? What were you afraid of—their reaction, losing the relationship, being seen as selfish or mean? What finally made you realize you had to do it anyway?

3. How did you communicate the boundary? Was it a conversation, an action, or both? What did you say or do to make it clear things were changing?

4. How did they react? Did they respect it, push back, try to negotiate, or act like you'd betrayed them? What was their immediate response?

5. Did you hold the boundary, or did you waver? Were there moments when you almost backed down? What kept you from giving in?

6. How did setting that boundary change your relationship with that person—or change you? Did things get better, worse, or just different? What did you learn about yourself from finally saying no?

Telling the Truth

"The truth will set you free, but first it will piss you off."

— Gloria Steinem

There comes a moment when keeping the peace costs more than telling the truth. You've been carrying a secret, holding back information, or letting someone believe a lie because the truth felt too dangerous, too hurtful, or too complicated. But secrets have weight, and eventually that weight becomes unbearable. So you made the decision to tell the truth, knowing it would change everything, and said it out loud anyway.

Maybe the truth was about you—something you'd been hiding about your past, your feelings, or a choice you made. Maybe it was about them—something you knew that they didn't, something you witnessed, or something you could no longer pretend not to see. Maybe it was a confession, a revelation, or just finally saying out loud what everyone already suspected but nobody wanted to acknowledge. Either way, once you said it, there was no taking it back.

The moment before you told the truth, you had a choice. You could've kept quiet, let things continue as they were, avoided the fallout. But something in you decided that honesty mattered more than comfort. Maybe you were tired of lying. Maybe you couldn't live with yourself if you stayed silent. Maybe you just reached a point where the truth felt like the only option, even if it cost you something.

What happened after you told the truth is the real story. Did they believe you? Thank you? Hate you for it? Did it destroy something, or did it clear the air and make room for something real? Did you regret saying it, or did you feel lighter for finally unburdening yourself? The truth changes things. This is the story of the truth you told, and what it cost you—or set you free from.

Writing Prompt Questions

1. What was the truth you finally told? What had you been hiding, holding back, or avoiding saying out loud for so long?

2. How long had you been carrying this truth before you finally spoke it? What made you decide that this was the moment to say it?

3. Who did you tell, and how did you do it? Was it planned or spontaneous? What words did you use, and where were you when you said it?

4. How did they react? Were they shocked, angry, relieved, or did they already know? What happened in the moments immediately after you spoke?

5. What did telling the truth cost you? Did it damage a relationship, change how people saw you, or create consequences you had to deal with? Or did it bring relief?

6. Looking back, do you regret telling the truth, or are you glad you did? What did you learn about yourself, honesty, or what really matters from finally speaking up?

Choosing Yourself

"Love yourself first and everything else falls into line."
— Lucille Ball

For most of your life, you probably put yourself last. You chose what was best for your kids, your partner, your parents, your job—everyone except yourself. You made yourself smaller, quieter, more convenient. You said yes when you meant no. You stayed when you wanted to leave. You sacrificed what you wanted for what other people needed. And then one day, you stopped. You made a choice that prioritized yourself, even though it disappointed or hurt someone else. You chose yourself, and everything changed.

Maybe it was a big choice—leaving a marriage, quitting a job, moving away from family, ending a friendship that had become toxic. Or maybe it was smaller but just as significant—saying no to an obligation, spending money on yourself without guilt, taking time you needed instead of giving it away. Whatever it was, the choice put your needs first, and that felt revolutionary because you'd spent so long pretending you didn't have any.

The guilt came immediately. You'd been conditioned to believe that choosing yourself was selfish, that good women sacrifice, that putting your needs first makes you a bad mother or daughter or partner. The voices in your head told you that you were wrong, that you should put everyone else first like you always had. But you held firm anyway, because something in you knew that you couldn't keep giving from an empty cup.

Choosing yourself changed your relationships. Some people respected it and adjusted. Others took it personally, as if your self-care was a rejection of them. But you survived their disappointment, and you discovered that you could prioritize yourself without the world falling apart. This is the story of the moment you chose yourself, and what you gained or lost by doing it.

Writing Prompt Questions

1. What choice did you make that put yourself first? What did you choose for yourself instead of choosing what others wanted or needed from you?

2. What made you finally do it? Was there a breaking point, a realization, or just exhaustion from always putting yourself last? What shifted?

3. Who were you disappointing or letting down by choosing yourself? What was their reaction when you made that choice?

4. What guilt or resistance did you feel? Did voices in your head tell you that you were being selfish? How did you push through that?

5. What did choosing yourself cost you? Did you lose relationships, face consequences, or deal with backlash? Was it worth it?

6. How did that choice change your life? What did you gain by finally prioritizing yourself? What do you wish you'd learned sooner about the importance of choosing yourself?

Defending Someone

"Courage is what it takes to stand up and speak."
— Winston Churchill

There's a moment when you see someone being attacked, criticized, or treated unfairly, and you have a choice: stay quiet and let it happen, or speak up and defend them. Maybe it was a friend being gossiped about, a coworker being blamed for something they didn't do, your kid being bullied, or a stranger being mistreated in public. You could've looked away, minded your business, told yourself it wasn't your problem. But you didn't. You stepped in and said something.

Defending someone isn't always dramatic. Sometimes it's quiet—a private conversation where you set the record straight, or refusing to participate when people are tearing someone down. Other times it's loud and public—calling someone out in the moment, standing physically between the aggressor and the victim, or making it clear that if they want to come after this person, they'll have to go through you first. Either way, you made yourself a target by choosing a side.

What makes defending someone meaningful is that you didn't have to do it. It wasn't your fight. You could've stayed silent and protected yourself. But something in you couldn't tolerate watching injustice happen without speaking up. Maybe you'd been in their position before and knew what it felt like to be alone. Maybe you just couldn't stomach cowardice. Whatever the reason, you chose courage over comfort.

The person you defended might have thanked you, or they might not have even known you did it. The people you stood up to might have backed down, or they might have turned on you instead. Either way, you proved something to yourself about what you stand for and who you are when someone needs an ally. This is the story of who you defended, and why it mattered.

Writing Prompt Questions

1. Who did you defend, and what were they being attacked for? Set the scene—what was happening, and who was coming after them?

2. Why did you feel compelled to step in? What was it about the situation that made you decide you couldn't stay silent?

3. What did you actually say or do to defend them? Was it a public confrontation, a private conversation, or just refusing to go along with the crowd?

4. How did the person or people you stood up to react? Did they back down, get defensive, or turn on you instead?

5. How did the person you defended respond? Did they thank you, or did they not even realize you'd stepped in? Did it change your relationship with them?

6. Looking back, was defending them worth whatever it cost you? Would you do it again? What did that moment teach you about standing up for others?

Breaking Family Silence

"The truth you speak has no past and no future. It just is."
— Richard Bach

Every family has secrets—the things nobody talks about, the truths everyone knows but pretends not to see. Maybe it's addiction, abuse, mental illness, infidelity, or just dysfunction so normalized that acknowledging it feels like betrayal. The unspoken rule is clear: we don't talk about this. And for years, maybe you followed that rule. You kept quiet, played along, protected the family image. Until one day, you didn't. You broke the silence and said out loud what everyone had been pretending wasn't real.

Breaking family silence is an act of defiance. You're not just telling a secret —you're violating the social contract that holds the family together through denial. Maybe you did it because you couldn't carry the weight anymore, or because staying silent felt like being complicit, or because someone needed to name the truth so healing could start. Maybe you did it out of anger, or desperation, or just exhaustion from pretending everything was fine when it absolutely wasn't.

What you said probably caused chaos. Some family members might have been relieved that someone finally said it. Others were furious that you broke ranks and exposed what was supposed to stay hidden. You might have been called a troublemaker, accused of airing dirty laundry, told you were destroying the family. The irony, of course, is that the secret was already destroying the family—you just made it visible.

Breaking the silence changed your position in the family forever. Maybe some relationships survived because honesty created space for real connection. Others didn't survive because they were built entirely on the mutual agreement to lie. Either way, you chose truth over peace, and that takes courage most people never have to find.

Writing Prompt Questions

1. What family secret did you break silence about? What had everyone been pretending wasn't happening, and what finally made you speak up?

2. How long had the silence been going on? Was this something hidden for years, or a recent issue everyone was already avoiding?

3. How did you break the silence—was it intentional and planned, or did it burst out in a moment of frustration? What did you actually say?

4. Who reacted with relief, and who reacted with anger? How did different family members respond to you naming the truth?

5. What consequences did you face for speaking up? Were you ostracized, blamed, cut off? Or did breaking the silence create space for healing?

6. Looking back, do you regret breaking the silence, or are you glad you did? What did you learn about your family, truth, and the cost of honesty?

Bridge Burned

"Sometimes you have to burn bridges to stop yourself from crossing them again."
— L.M. Browning

Most of the time, we're taught to leave doors open, to never burn bridges, to keep things civil just in case. But sometimes, burning the bridge is the healthiest thing you can do. Not in anger, not out of spite, but as a deliberate decision to make sure you can't go back to something that wasn't good for you. Maybe it was a friendship that had become toxic, a job that was destroying you, a relationship you kept returning to even though you knew better, or a family dynamic you finally walked away from. You didn't just leave—you made it so you couldn't come back.

Burning a bridge on purpose is different from things ending badly. It's intentional. You're not slamming a door in rage—you're closing it, locking it, and removing the key. Maybe you said what needed to be said and didn't soften it. Maybe you walked away mid-conversation and never looked back. Maybe you cut contact completely, blocked numbers, made it clear there would be no reconciliation. You knew people would call you cold, unforgiving, harsh. You did it anyway.

The thing about burning bridges is that it forces you forward. You can't second-guess yourself at 2 a.m. and reach out. You can't fall back into old patterns when things get hard. You made a clean break, and the finality of it was the point. Some people understood. Others thought you were cruel. But you weren't doing it to hurt anyone—you were doing it to protect yourself.

That bridge needed to burn. Looking back, you'd light the match again. This is the story of what you walked away from, and why you made sure you could never go back.

Writing Prompt Questions

1. What bridge did you burn, and why did it need to burn? Who or what were you cutting off, and what made you decide a clean break was the only option?

2. How did you do it—what was the final conversation, message, or action that made it clear you were done? Did you explain yourself, or did you just disappear? What did you say or do to make it permanent?

3. Was it premeditated, or did it happen in the heat of a moment? Had you been thinking about it for a while, or did something push you over the edge and you acted immediately?

4. How did they react when they realized you weren't coming back? Did they try to reach out? Apologize? Get angry? Or did they accept it and move on?

5. Did anyone judge you for burning that bridge? Were there people who thought you should've forgiven, tried harder, or kept the peace? How did you handle their opinions?

6. Do you regret it, or was it one of the best decisions you ever made? Looking back now, would you do it again, or do you wish you'd handled it differently?

Refusing to Apologize

"Never apologize for being yourself."
— Paulo Coelho

There's a difference between apologizing because you genuinely did something wrong, and apologizing just to smooth things over. For too long, maybe you were the person who always said sorry—sorry for speaking up, sorry for taking up space, sorry for having needs or opinions. You apologized reflexively, even when you weren't wrong, because it was easier than conflict. Until one day, someone expected an apology and you refused to give it. You stood your ground and said no, I'm not sorry, and you meant it.

Maybe they expected you to apologize for setting a boundary, or for choosing yourself, or for telling a truth they didn't want to hear. Maybe they thought if they made enough noise or acted hurt enough, you'd cave like you always had. But this time, you didn't. You looked at what they were asking you to apologize for and realized that doing so would mean denying your own worth, your own truth, or your own right to exist as you are.

Refusing to apologize when someone expects it creates tension. They might have escalated—gotten angrier, accused you of being stubborn or cruel, weaponized your refusal to make you look like the villain. Maybe other people got involved, trying to convince you to just say sorry and make peace. But you held firm, because apologizing would have meant accepting blame for something that wasn't your fault, or shrinking yourself to make someone else comfortable.

That refusal to apologize was an act of self-respect. It said: I will not be sorry for being myself, for having boundaries, for telling the truth. Some relationships couldn't survive your refusal to back down. Others became healthier because you stopped performing apologies you didn't mean. This is the story of what you refused to apologize for, and why.

Writing Prompt Questions

1. What did someone want you to apologize for, and why did you refuse? What were they demanding an apology for, and why wasn't it yours to give?

2. What made you decide not to apologize? Was it principle, exhaustion from always being the one who apologized, or the realization that you'd done nothing wrong?

3. How did they react when you refused? Did they escalate, try to guilt you, or enlist others to pressure you? What tactics did they use?

4. Did anyone else get involved and try to convince you to apologize "for the sake of peace"? How did you handle that pressure?

5. What did it feel like to stand your ground? Was it empowering, terrifying, or both? Did you doubt yourself, or were you certain you were right?

6. Looking back, are you glad you didn't apologize? Did refusing to say sorry change your relationship with that person, or change how you see yourself? What did it teach you about standing firm?

Standing Up to Someone

"Be a voice, not an echo."
— Albert Einstein

There comes a moment when you've had enough. When you've bitten your tongue one too many times, swallowed your words to keep the peace, or let something slide that shouldn't have slid. And then, something shifts. Maybe it was something they said, or the way they said it, or the fact that they'd gotten away with it for too long. Whatever it was, you decided right then that you were done staying quiet. You were going to say what needed to be said, consequences be damned.

Standing up to someone isn't always dramatic. Sometimes it's quiet and controlled—a firm "no" when you've always said yes, a boundary drawn after years of letting it get crossed. Other times it's explosive—the moment you finally snapped and let everything you'd been holding back come pouring out. Either way, it's the moment you chose your own voice over keeping someone else comfortable, and that choice changed something in you.

Maybe it was a boss who pushed too far, a family member who'd been taking advantage of you, a friend who crossed a line, or a stranger who said something that made your blood boil. Maybe people around you were shocked because you'd never been that person before. Or maybe they'd been waiting for you to finally do it, wondering how long you'd let it go on.

The moment after you stood up for yourself—when your heart was pounding and you weren't sure if you'd just made everything better or worse—that moment matters. Because you proved to yourself that you could do it. That your voice mattered. That you were done shrinking. This is the story of who you stood up to, what you said, and what happened when you finally refused to back down.

Writing Prompt Questions

1. Who did you stand up to, and what pattern had you been tolerating? How long had this been building before you finally hit your breaking point?

2. What was the final straw—the specific moment or thing they did that made you say 'enough'? What happened right before you stood up to them?

3. What did you actually say? Can you remember the words you used? Was it planned, or did it come out in the heat of the moment? Did you say everything you wanted to say, or did you hold some back?

4. Was anyone else there to witness it? How did they react—did they support you, stay silent, or try to smooth things over? Did their response surprise you?

5. What did it feel like after you did it? Relief? Fear? Regret? Empowerment? How long did it take for your hands to stop shaking?

6. Did standing up to them change your relationship, or change you? Did things get better, worse, or just different? What did you learn about yourself from finally speaking up?

Risk & Adventure

6 Memory Sparks

A Trip That Changed You

"Not all who wander are lost."
— J.R.R. Tolkien

Some trips are just vacations—you go, you see things, rest a little, then come home. And then there are the trips that crack you open, the ones where you leave as one version of yourself and come back as someone slightly different. Maybe it was your first time out of the country, or just the first time away from home without your parents watching. Maybe it was a summer in Europe, a semester abroad, a road trip with friends, or three months working at a beach town where nobody knew your name.

The destination matters less than what happened to you there. Maybe you were nineteen in Paris, dancing in clubs until dawn and realizing the world was bigger and stranger than your hometown ever let on. Maybe you were twenty-two and drove cross-country with two friends in a car that barely made it. Maybe you spent a summer waitressing in a coastal town and fell in love with someone you knew you'd never see again. Maybe you went somewhere to find yourself and actually did.

Travel changes you because it takes you out of the story you've been living and drops you into a new one. Different rules, different people, different possibilities. You do things you'd never do at home. You talk to strangers. You stay up all night. You say yes to things that scare you. You become braver, or lonelier, or more alive, or all three at once.

This is the trip that left a mark—the one you still think about when you're stuck in traffic or doing dishes. The place that made you different. The journey that reminded you who you actually were, or could be. This is the story of where you went, who you became there, and what you brought back with you.

Writing Prompt Questions

1. Where did you go, and what made you decide to go there? Was it planned or impulsive? What were you hoping to find?

2. Describe the moment you realized this trip was different from anything you'd done before. What happened that made you feel like you'd stepped into a new version of your life?

3. Who did you meet on this trip that you still think about? A fellow traveler, a local, someone you spent three days with and never saw again? What did they teach you or show you?

4. What did you do on that trip that you never would have done at home? Did you take a risk, break a rule, try something completely out of character?

5. Was there a moment on that trip when you felt completely free, completely yourself, or completely alive? Describe what you were doing, where you were, and what that feeling was like.

6. How were you different when you came home? What did you bring back with you that wasn't a souvenir—a new perspective, a secret, a story you knew would sound unbelievable if you told it?

Your Favorite Car

"Life is a journey, not a destination."
— Ralph Waldo Emerson

Cars are never just cars. They're where life happens—the conversations, the road trips, the first kiss in the back seat, the drives with nowhere to go but away. The best car you ever owned wasn't necessarily the nicest or the newest. It was the one that got you where you needed to be, literally and figuratively. It was the car that saw you through a specific chapter of your life, and every time you see one like it on the road, you're nineteen again, windows down, music too loud, convinced you're invincible.

Maybe it was your first car—a hand-me-down with a busted radio and a passenger door that didn't lock, but it was yours and that's all that mattered. Maybe it was the car you drove cross-country, or the one you learned to drive stick in, stalling out at every stoplight until you finally figured it out. Maybe it was the car you bought with your own money, the one that represented freedom, independence, and the fact that you didn't need anyone's permission to go wherever you wanted.

That car had a personality. It had quirks—the way you had to jiggle the key, the spot on the floor where the carpet was worn through, the smell of it that you can still conjure if you think hard enough. It had a soundtrack, too. The songs you played on repeat, the late-night drives with friends, the moments of silence when you just needed to think.

You remember that car better than you remember most people from that time. It wasn't just transportation. It was a witness to who you were and who you were becoming. This is the story of the car that mattered, the places it took you, and the memories you made inside it.

Writing Prompt Questions

1. What kind of car was it, and how did it become yours? Did you buy it, inherit it, borrow it indefinitely? What year, make, and model—and what condition was it in when you got it?

2. What were its quirks? The broken air conditioning, the radio stuck on one station, the driver's seat that leaned too far back? What did you have to know to drive it that no one else knew?

3. Where did that car take you? Was there a specific road trip, a daily commute, a late-night escape? What's the most memorable drive you took in it?

4. Where did that car take you? Was there a specific road trip, a daily commute, a late-night escape? What's the most memorable drive you took in it?

5. What was always playing on the radio or tape deck? What songs are permanently linked to that car in your memory? Can you still hear them when you picture yourself behind the wheel?

6. How did you lose it—sell it, wreck it, run it into the ground? Do you wish you still had it, or was it time to let it go? If you saw that exact car today, would you want it back?

The Concert

"Music is the shorthand of emotion."
— Leo Tolstoy

There are concerts you go to, and then there are concerts that become part of your origin story. The ones where the music was so loud you felt it in your chest, where the crowd moved as one organism, where you screamed lyrics until your voice gave out and didn't care. The show where you weren't just watching—you were part of something bigger, something electric, something you knew even in the moment you'd remember for the rest of your life.

Maybe it was a band you'd loved for years finally coming to your town, or a festival where you discovered someone new and had your mind blown. Maybe you were front row, or you snuck backstage, or you were in the nosebleeds but it didn't matter because the energy was everywhere. Maybe you drove hours to get there, camped out for tickets, or bought them on a whim and had no idea what you were walking into. Either way, that night rewired something in you.

The details are visceral. What you wore. Who you went with. The opening band you'd never heard of that turned out to be incredible. The moment the lights went down and the crowd lost it. The song that hit different live than it ever did on the radio. The stranger next to you who became your best friend for two hours. The drive home where you couldn't stop talking about what you'd just witnessed.

Music marks time in a way nothing else does. You hear a song from that concert and you're twenty-two again, immortal, convinced that night would never end. This is the story of the concert that changed you, the one that made you feel completely alive.

Writing Prompt Questions

1. Who did you see, and where was the concert? What band or artist? What venue? How old were you, and why did this show matter so much?

2. Who did you go with, and what do you remember about getting there? The road trip, the anticipation, the moment you walked into the venue? What was the energy like before the music even started?

3. What song or moment from that concert is burned into your memory? Was there a song where the entire crowd sang along? A moment where you lost your mind? Describe what you felt.

4. Did anything unexpected happen that night? Did you meet someone, see something wild, have an experience that became part of the legend of that show?

5. What were you wearing, and can you still picture exactly how you looked that night? Sometimes the outfit is part of the memory. What did you wear, and why?

6. How did that concert change you, or what did it represent in your life at that time? Was it freedom, rebellion, joy, or just a perfect night you wish you could live again?

The Move

"Sometimes the hardest part isn't letting go but rather learning to start over."
— Nicole Sobon

Moving isn't just about changing addresses—it's about leaving behind a version of your life and starting over somewhere new. Maybe it was a move across the country, to a different state, or just across town, but it changed everything. You left behind friends, routines, the places you knew by heart, and walked into uncertainty. Maybe you moved for a job, for love, to escape something, or just because you needed a fresh start. Either way, you packed up your life and bet on the possibility that somewhere else could be better.

The decision to move is rarely easy. Maybe you agonized over it for months, weighing pros and cons, talking yourself in and out of it. Or maybe you made the choice impulsively, signed a lease or accepted a job offer before you could talk yourself out of it. Maybe people told you that you were brave, or crazy, or making a mistake. Maybe you weren't sure yourself until you were already there, unpacking boxes in a place that didn't feel like home yet.

The first few weeks in a new place are disorienting. Everything is unfamiliar—the streets, the stores, the rhythms of daily life. You don't know anyone, or you only know one person and they're the reason you moved. You question whether you made the right choice. You miss what you left behind, even the parts you hated. And then slowly, things shift. You find your favorite coffee shop, make a friend, discover a routine. The new place starts to feel less foreign.

That move changed you. Maybe it gave you exactly what you were looking for, or maybe it taught you something unexpected. Maybe you're still there, or maybe you left and went somewhere else. Either way, this is the story of the move that mattered.

Writing Prompt Questions

1. Where did you move from and where did you go? What prompted the move—a job, a relationship, escape, adventure, or something else?

2. What was the hardest part about deciding to move? What were you leaving behind, and what were you hoping to find? What made you finally commit to going?

3. What do you remember about the actual move itself? The packing, the drive or flight, the first night in the new place? What did it feel like to arrive?

4. What was the hardest adjustment in those first weeks or months? What did you miss most about where you came from? When did the new place start to feel like home, if it ever did?

5. Did the move give you what you were looking for, or did you discover something completely different? How did it change your life or change you?

6. Looking back, was moving the right decision? Do you have any regrets, or are you glad you took the risk? What did that move teach you about yourself and what you're capable of?

Skinny Dipping

"You only live once, but if you do it right, once is enough."
— Mae West

There's something liberating about being naked in water under the open sky. Maybe it was a lake at midnight, or the ocean at dawn, or a friend's pool when everyone had too much to drink and someone dared everyone else to strip down and jump in. Whatever the circumstances, skinny dipping wasn't just about swimming—it was about shedding inhibitions along with your clothes and feeling completely, recklessly free.

The decision to do it probably came fast. Someone suggested it, and before you could overthink it, you were pulling off your shirt and running toward the water. Maybe you were with people you trusted completely, or maybe you were with near-strangers and the anonymity made it easier. Maybe it was planned, or maybe it was spontaneous—one of those "why not?" moments that defines a night. Either way, once you were in the water, naked and laughing, you felt alive in a way you hadn't in a long time.

There's vulnerability in skinny dipping, but also power. You're exposed, but so is everyone else. You're breaking a rule—public nudity, trespassing, or just doing something your parents would've killed you for. The risk of getting caught made it more thrilling. Maybe someone did catch you—a neighbor, a cop, someone walking by—and you had to scramble for your clothes while trying not to laugh. Or maybe you got away with it, and that made it even better.

Skinny dipping stays with you because it's one of those rare moments where you're completely present—feeling the water on your skin, the night air, the rush of doing something just because you can. This is the story of the night you stripped down and jumped in.

Writing Prompt Questions

1. Where were you, and whose idea was it? A lake, ocean, pool, river? How did the idea come up, and what made you decide to actually do it?

2. Who were you with? Friends, strangers, a romantic partner, or were you alone? How did the group dynamic affect the experience?

3. What was the moment like right before you got in? Were you nervous, excited, self-conscious? What did it feel like to take your clothes off?

4. What do you remember about being in the water? The temperature, the feeling, the conversation or laughter? What made it memorable beyond just being naked?

5. Did you almost get caught, or did you actually get caught? What happened, and how did you handle it? Or did you get away clean?

6. Looking back, what did that experience represent? Freedom, rebellion, youth, connection? Would you do it again, or was it perfect as a one-time thing?

Learning to Drive

"Adventure is worthwhile in itself."
— Amelia Earhart

Learning to drive wasn't just about mastering a vehicle—it was about freedom, independence, and proof that you were becoming someone who could go anywhere without asking permission. Maybe you learned at sixteen with a parent in the passenger seat gripping the door handle, or maybe you were older and finally decided it was time to stop relying on other people for rides. Either way, the moment you got behind the wheel for the first time, everything felt both terrifying and thrilling.

The person teaching you matters almost as much as the learning itself. Maybe it was your dad who stayed calm while you jerked through stop signs, or your mom who yelled every time you got too close to the curb. Maybe it was a driving instructor who'd seen it all and somehow stayed patient, or a boyfriend who thought he could teach you and immediately regretted it. Whoever it was, they witnessed you at your most nervous—sweating, overthinking every movement, convinced you were going to hit something or stall out in the middle of an intersection.

Learning stick shift was its own special hell if you went that route. The coordination required—clutch, gas, shift, don't roll backwards on a hill—felt impossible at first. You stalled out at red lights while cars honked behind you. You ground the gears so badly you were sure you'd destroyed the transmission. And then one day, it just clicked, and suddenly you were driving like you'd been born doing it.

The first time you drove alone—no adult, no instructor, just you and the open road—you felt invincible. You could go anywhere. You weren't trapped at home waiting for someone to take you somewhere. You had wheels, and that changed everything.

Writing Prompt Questions

1. How old were you when you learned to drive, and who taught you? What kind of car did you learn in, and what do you remember about those first lessons?

2. What was the hardest part of learning—parallel parking, merging, stick shift, staying calm? What were you convinced you'd never be able to master?

3. Was there a memorable disaster during your learning process? Did you hit something, stall out somewhere embarrassing, or have a moment when you thought you'd never get your license?

4. Describe your driving test. Did you pass the first time or have to retake it? What happened, and how did you feel when you finally got your license?

5. What was the first place you drove to alone after getting your license? Where did you go, and what did that freedom feel like?

6. How did learning to drive change your life? What did having a license and the ability to drive give you that you didn't have before? What did that independence mean to you?

Body & Physicality

6 Memory Sparks

Physical Strength

"Strong women don't have attitudes. They have standards."
— Marilyn Monroe

There's a moment when you discover your own physical strength—not just that you have it, but that you can actually use it when it matters. Maybe it was moving furniture by yourself when no one else was there to help, lifting something you didn't think you could, or physically doing something that proved you were stronger than you looked. Maybe it was childbirth, where your body did something impossible and survived. Maybe it was defending someone, standing your ground physically, or just refusing to be moved when someone tried to push you around.

The moment you realized your own strength probably surprised you. You didn't know you had it in you until circumstances demanded it and you rose to meet them. Maybe you were angry, or desperate, or just determined not to ask for help. Maybe someone underestimated you and you proved them spectacularly wrong. Either way, your body did something that changed how you saw yourself—you weren't fragile, you weren't weak, you were capable of more than you'd been told.

What makes physical strength meaningful isn't just having it—it's using it when it counts. Maybe you carried your sleeping child up three flights of stairs, or moved an entire household by yourself, or fought back against someone who thought they could overpower you. Maybe you worked a physically demanding job and kept up with the men who assumed you couldn't. Maybe you survived something that tested every ounce of strength you had and came out the other side standing.

That moment when you felt your own power—in your arms, your legs, your core, your sheer refusal to give up—stays with you. This is the story of when your body proved what it could do.

Writing Prompt Questions

1. What moment revealed your physical strength? What were you doing that required strength you didn't know you had, or weren't sure you possessed?

2. What prompted it—necessity, anger, determination, emergency? What made you dig deep and find that strength?

3. Did anyone witness it, and were they surprised? Did someone underestimate you and watch you prove them wrong? What was their reaction?

4. What did it feel like in your body to do that thing? Describe the physical sensation—the burn, the power, the moment you realized you could actually do it.

5. How did discovering or using that strength change how you saw yourself? Did it make you feel more capable, more confident, or just surprised at what your body could handle?

6. Looking back, what does that moment of physical strength represent to you? What did it teach you about your own capabilities or what you're made of?

The Scar

"Scars are just tattoos with better stories."
— Unknown

Every scar tells a story, and some stories are worth telling. Maybe it's visible—on your face, your arm, somewhere people can see and ask about. Or maybe it's hidden, something only you and a few people know exists. Either way, that scar is a permanent mark, a reminder of a moment when your body broke and then healed itself back together. The story of how you got it says something about who you were, what you survived, or what you were willing to risk.

Maybe you got the scar from an accident—a car crash, a fall, something that happened so fast you didn't have time to protect yourself. Maybe it was from a fight, a surgical procedure, or an injury doing something reckless that seemed like a good idea at the time. Maybe you were a kid and the scar has been with you so long it feels like part of your identity. Or maybe you got it as an adult and it marked a turning point, a before and after in your life.

Scars carry weight beyond the physical mark. People ask about them, make assumptions, tell you what they think happened. Some scars you're proud of—proof you survived something, evidence of your strength. Others you wish you could erase, reminders of pain or mistakes or moments you'd rather forget. Either way, the scar is there, and it's not going anywhere.

What happened that day when your skin broke open? What were you doing, and why? Did it hurt as much as you thought it would, or were you too shocked to feel it right away? And now, years later, when you look at that scar, what do you think? This is the story of the mark you carry and what it cost you to get it.

Writing Prompt Questions

1. How did you get the scar? What happened—an accident, a fight, an injury, a surgery? Set the scene and walk us through the moment your body was marked permanently.

2. How bad was it at the time? Did you need stitches, surgery, or did it heal on its own? What was the immediate aftermath like?

3. If it was from surgery, what was that experience like? The decision to go under the knife, the fear, the recovery? How did the surgical scar become part of your story?

4. Where is the scar, and can people see it? Do strangers ask about it, or is it something only certain people know exists? How do you feel when people notice it?

5. What does that scar represent to you now? Is it a badge of honor, a reminder of survival, or something you wish you could erase? Has your relationship with it changed over time?

6. If that scar could talk, what story would it tell about who you were when you got it? What does it say about what you've survived or what you were willing to risk?

The Fight

"I'm not a do-nothing bitch."
— Ronda Rousey

Most people go their whole lives without throwing a punch or taking one. But there's a moment when words aren't enough, when something in you snaps, and suddenly you're in a physical fight. Maybe it was self-defense—someone came at you and you fought back. Maybe it was defending someone else who couldn't defend themselves. Or maybe it was pure rage—someone pushed you too far and your body reacted before your brain could stop it. Either way, you crossed a line you can't uncross, and everything happened fast.

The moment before a fight is electric. Your heart is pounding, your hands are shaking, adrenaline floods your system. Maybe you tried to walk away and they wouldn't let you. Maybe you knew it was coming and braced for it. Or maybe it erupted out of nowhere—one second you're arguing, the next second someone's grabbed you or you've grabbed them. The first physical contact changes everything. Once it starts, there's no thinking, just reacting.

What happened during the fight is probably a blur. Maybe you remember specific details—the sound of impact, the pain, the shock of how much it hurt or how much you were capable of hurting someone else. Maybe you won, or lost, or it got broken up before either of you could claim victory. Maybe you walked away with bruises, or a black eye, or just shaking hands and the knowledge that you'd actually done it.

The aftermath of a fight stays with you. Maybe you felt powerful, or horrified, or both. Maybe there were consequences—legal, social, physical. Maybe people saw you differently after, or you saw yourself differently. This is the story of the fight, and what it taught you about your own capacity for violence.

Writing Prompt Questions

1. What led to the fight? Set the scene—who were you fighting, where were you, and what pushed it from words to physical violence?

2. Who threw the first punch, or made the first physical move? Was it you, or were you reacting to them? What was that moment like?

3. What do you remember about the actual fight? The specific blows, the pain, the chaos? Or is it mostly a blur of adrenaline and motion?

4. How did it end? Did someone break it up, did one of you back down, or did you fight until you couldn't anymore? What stopped it?

5. What were the consequences? Injuries, trouble with the law, damaged relationships, reputation changes? What did that fight cost you?

6. Looking back, do you regret it, or are you glad you fought? What did that physical confrontation teach you about yourself—your limits, your strength, or your capacity for violence?

Miscarriage or Loss

"Grief is the price we pay for love."
— Queen Elizabeth II

Losing a pregnancy is a kind of loss that doesn't get talked about enough. One day you're pregnant, planning a future, imagining a person. The next day, or week, that future is gone. Maybe it happened early, before you'd told anyone, and you grieved alone. Maybe it happened later, after you'd seen ultrasounds and heard a heartbeat and started to believe it was real. Either way, the loss is real, even if the baby never was to the outside world.

The moment you knew something was wrong is burned into memory. Maybe it was bleeding, cramping, or just a sudden absence of the symptoms you'd been tracking. Maybe a doctor delivered the news with clinical detachment, or with compassion, but either way the words landed like a bomb. No heartbeat. I'm sorry. These things happen. As if that made it hurt less.

What came after was both physical and emotional. The pain of your body expelling what it had been growing. The decisions about how to handle it—naturally, with medication, with a procedure. The emptiness after, not just in your body but in the future you'd been building in your head. Maybe people said unhelpful things trying to comfort you. Maybe they avoided you because they didn't know what to say. Maybe you had to go back to work and pretend you were fine when you were falling apart.

Miscarriage and loss don't always get acknowledged as the grief they are. People move on quickly, expect you to try again, don't understand why you're still sad about something that wasn't even born yet. But you know what you lost—not just a pregnancy, but a person you'd already started to love.

Writing Prompt Questions

1. When did you lose the pregnancy, and how did you find out? What were the signs that something was wrong, or how did you get the news?

2. What was the physical experience like? The pain, the procedures, the aftermath? What do you remember about what your body went through?

3. How far along were you, and what did that pregnancy mean to you? Had you told people, made plans, started to imagine that child's life?

4. Who supported you through it, and who didn't? Were there people who showed up in ways you didn't expect, or people who disappeared when you needed them?

5. What did people say that helped or hurt? Were there comments that stuck with you—good or bad—in the aftermath of the loss?

6. How did that loss change you, your relationship with pregnancy, or your understanding of grief? What do you wish people understood about miscarriage that they don't?

Getting Your Period

"A woman is the full circle. Within her is the power to create, nurture and transform." — Diane Mariechild

Getting your period for the first time is supposed to mark your passage into womanhood, but nobody tells you it mostly just feels confusing, inconvenient, and kind of embarrassing. Maybe you were prepared—your mom had talked to you about it, you'd seen the videos in health class, you knew it was coming. Or maybe it caught you completely off guard, and suddenly you were dealing with blood and cramps and had no idea what was happening to your body.

The moment you realized it had started is burned into memory. Maybe you were at home and could quietly handle it, or maybe you were at school and had to figure it out in a public bathroom with nothing but toilet paper and panic. Maybe someone noticed before you did—a friend who quietly told you, or worse, a boy who pointed it out. Maybe you told your mom right away, or maybe you hid it for days because you weren't ready to deal with the conversation or the fuss.

What you felt about getting your period probably wasn't what the books said you'd feel. Maybe you felt grown up and proud, or maybe you felt betrayed by your body for making you deal with this every month for the rest of your fertile life. Maybe you were excited because your friends already had theirs and you felt left behind. Or maybe you were the first one in your group and felt weirdly isolated, dealing with something none of them understood yet.

That first period changed your relationship with your body. Suddenly you had to think about things you'd never thought about before—pads, tampons, cramps, tracking cycles, planning around it. Your body had its own agenda now, and you had to learn to navigate that whether you liked it or not.

Writing Prompt Questions

1. How old were you when you got your first period, and where were you when it happened? Were you at home, at school, or somewhere else? Describe the moment you realized it had started.

2. Were you prepared for it, or did it catch you completely off guard? Had anyone talked to you about periods, or were you figuring it out on your own?

3. How did you handle it in that moment? Did you know what to do, or did you have to ask for help? Who helped you, if anyone?

4. Who did you tell first, and how did that conversation go? Was it your mom, a friend, a sister? Or did you try to hide it for a while?

5. How did you feel about getting your period—excited, embarrassed, angry, or something else? Did it make you feel older, or just annoyed?

6. Looking back, what do you remember most about that experience? How did getting your period change how you thought about your body or growing up?

The Surgery

"The wound is the place where the Light enters you."
— Rumi

Going under the knife is terrifying no matter how routine the doctors say the procedure is. Maybe it was something minor—getting your wisdom teeth out, a knee surgery, something that thousands of people have done without issue. Or maybe it was major—an emergency operation, something life-threatening, a procedure that would change your body permanently. Either way, the moment they wheeled you into that operating room, you had to surrender complete control and trust that you'd wake up on the other side.

The decision to have surgery wasn't always yours. Maybe it was medically necessary and you had no choice, or maybe you'd been putting it off until the pain or the problem became unbearable. Maybe it was elective—something you chose to fix or change about your body. Whatever the reason, the days leading up to it were probably filled with anxiety, paperwork, pre-op appointments, and instructions about what you couldn't eat or drink. You had to get your affairs in order, tell people where you'd be, and hope that everything would go according to plan.

The surgery itself is mostly a blank in your memory—anesthesia does that. What you remember is before and after. The cold operating room. The IV going in. The anesthesiologist telling you to count backwards. And then nothing. And then waking up in recovery, disoriented and in pain, trying to piece together what happened while you were gone. Maybe the surgery went perfectly, or maybe there were complications. Maybe recovery was easier than you expected, or maybe it was brutal.

That surgery left a mark—literally, in the form of a scar, and figuratively in how it changed your body or your life. This is the story of going under and coming back.

Writing Prompt Questions

1. What was the surgery for, and was it elective or necessary? What led to you needing or choosing to have it? How old were you?

2. What do you remember about the days leading up to it? Were you scared, anxious, in denial? What was going through your mind before you went in?

3. Describe the moments right before the surgery. What do you remember about being prepped, the operating room, the moment before anesthesia took over?

4. What was waking up like? Where were you, how did you feel, and what was the first thing you remember after coming out of anesthesia?

5. How was the recovery—physical and emotional? Was it harder or easier than you expected? What was the worst part of healing?

6. How did that surgery change your body or your life? What's different now because you had it? Do you have regrets, or are you glad you did it?

Money & Power

3 Memory Sparks

The Business

"I never dreamed about success. I worked for it."
— Estée Lauder

Some women dream about starting a business. Others just do it. Maybe you were one who actually took the leap—sold crafts at flea markets, started a catering business out of your kitchen, opened a boutique, or ran a service nobody else was offering. Or maybe you had an idea that stayed an idea, something you thought about for years but never quite pulled the trigger on. Either story is worth telling—the one where you tried, or the one where you didn't and still wonder "what if?"

If you did it, you know what it took. The guts to believe your idea was worth pursuing, the scramble to figure out things you had no training for, the days you felt brilliant and the days you wondered what you'd gotten yourself into. You made business cards, set prices, dealt with customers, handled money, and learned on the fly. You negotiated with suppliers, stayed up late doing bookkeeping, and made a thousand decisions without a safety net. Maybe it succeeded beyond your expectations. Maybe it failed spectacularly. Maybe it taught you expensive lessons about business, money, and yourself. But you tried, and that matters more than whether it worked.

If you didn't do it, there's a reason. Maybe the timing was never right, or the risk felt too big, or life got in the way. Maybe you talked yourself out of it, or someone else did. Maybe you still think about it—the boutique you would've opened, the service you would've offered, the thing you knew you could do better than anyone else if you'd just had the chance. That unlaunched business lives in your mind as both regret and possibility.

Whether you started it or didn't, that business idea says something about who you were and what you wanted. Both stories—the one where you went for it and the one where you held back—are worth exploring. This is the story of the business you built or the one that got away.

Writing Prompt Questions

1. What was the business idea—what were you going to sell, offer, or create? Where did the idea come from, and what made you think it could work?

2. If you started it: How did you actually get it off the ground? What were the first steps, and what was harder than you expected? If you didn't start it: What stopped you—fear, money, timing, someone's opinion?

3. If you started it: What was your best day or biggest win? A sale, a customer, a moment of validation? If you didn't start it: What would success have looked like if you'd gone for it?

4. If you started it: How did it end, or is it still going? What made you close it, sell it, or walk away? If you didn't start it: Do you still think about it, or have you made peace with not doing it?

5. What did that business (real or imagined) represent to you? Independence? Creativity? Proof of something? What would having it have meant?

6. If you could go back, would you do anything differently? Start it if you didn't? Do it differently if you did? Or leave it exactly as it is—pursued or unpursued?

The Side Hustle

"Work hard in silence, let your success be the noise."
— Frank Ocean

You had a life everyone could see—the job, the family, the routine. But you also had something else, something you kept quiet about. Maybe it was a side hustle that brought in extra cash, or a creative project you poured yourself into after everyone went to bed, or a skill you monetized without making a big announcement. Maybe you kept it secret because you weren't sure it would work, or because you didn't want to hear opinions, or because it was yours and you liked having something that belonged only to you.

Some side hustles are practical—selling things online, freelancing, picking up shifts nobody knew about. Others are more personal—writing, creating, building something that mattered to you even if it never made much money. Either way, you were doing something outside the main narrative of your life, and most people had no idea. You had a whole other operation running in the margins, funded by your own time and energy and determination.

Maybe you kept it secret because you were embarrassed, or because it felt too vulnerable to share before it was proven. Maybe you didn't want judgment or advice or people asking how it was going every time you saw them. Or maybe you just liked the autonomy—the freedom to try, fail, pivot, or succeed without an audience weighing in. It was your experiment, your gamble, your late-night project that no one else had to understand.

Eventually, some people found out. Or maybe they never did, and it stayed your private thing—the part of your life you controlled completely. Maybe it grew into something bigger than you expected, or maybe it stayed small and personal. Maybe you still do it, or maybe it served its purpose and you moved on. Either way, that side hustle was yours in a way few things in life are, and it taught you what you're capable of when no one's watching.

Writing Prompt Questions

1. What was the side hustle, and how did you get started? What were you doing, how did you learn to do it, and what made you think you could make it work?

2. When and where did you work on it? Early mornings, late nights, lunch breaks? Where did you carve out the time and space to make it happen?

3. Why did you keep it quiet? Were you protecting it, embarrassed by it, or just enjoying having something that was entirely yours? Who knew about it, if anyone?

4. Did it make money, and if so, what did you do with it? Was it pocket money, savings, something you spent on yourself without asking permission? What did that financial independence feel like?

5. How did people react when they found out (if they ever did)? Were they surprised, supportive, dismissive? Did anyone say "I had no idea you were doing that"?

6. Do you still do it, or did it run its course? If you stopped, why? If you're still doing it, what has it become? What did having that side hustle teach you about yourself?

Financial Independence

"A woman must have money and a room of her own."
— Virginia Woolf

There's a specific kind of freedom that comes with having your own money. Not household money, not money you have to justify spending, but money that's yours—earned by you, controlled by you, spent however you see fit without asking permission or explaining yourself. Maybe you achieved financial independence through a job, a business, an inheritance, or just years of careful saving. However it happened, the moment you realized you didn't need anyone else's money to survive changed everything.

Financial independence isn't always about being rich—it's about autonomy. Maybe it meant you could finally leave a bad relationship because you weren't financially trapped. Maybe it meant you could make decisions without consulting someone else's bank account. Maybe it just meant you could buy what you wanted without guilt or justification. For the first time, money wasn't something you had to negotiate for or depend on someone else to provide.

Getting to financial independence required sacrifice. Maybe you worked multiple jobs, lived lean, saved aggressively, or built something from nothing. Maybe you fought for equal pay, demanded what you were worth, or walked away from situations where you were undervalued. Maybe it took years longer than you wanted, but you stuck with it because the alternative—depending on someone else—felt like giving up a piece of yourself.

Once you had it, financial independence changed how you moved through the world. You could take risks because you had a safety net. You could say no because you didn't need the money badly enough to tolerate bad treatment. Money became freedom, and freedom became power. This is the story of how you got your own money and what it gave you beyond dollars in the bank.

Writing Prompt Questions

1. When did you achieve financial independence, and how did you get there? What job, decision, or circumstance gave you control over your own money for the first time?

2. What did financial independence mean to you—was it about survival, freedom, power, or something else? What could you finally do once you had your own money?

3. What did you have to sacrifice or give up to achieve financial independence? Long hours, lifestyle choices, relationships? What did it cost you to get there?

4. Was there a specific moment when you realized you were financially independent? A decision you could make, a purchase you could afford, or a situation you could walk away from? What did that feel like?

5. How did having your own money change your relationships—with partners, family, or friends? Did it shift power dynamics or create tension?

6. Looking back, what does financial independence represent to you now? What did having control over your own money teach you about power, freedom, and what really matters?

Survival & Lessons

5 Memory Sparks

What You Survived

"What doesn't kill you doesn't kill you."
— Serena Zhang

Some experiences don't just challenge you—they test whether you'll make it through at all. Maybe it was abuse, addiction, loss, trauma, illness, or a period of your life so dark you weren't sure you'd see the other side. Maybe it was something that happened to you, or something you did to yourself, or just circumstances that piled up until you were buried under the weight of them. Either way, you survived something that could have destroyed you, and the fact that you're still here means something.

Survival isn't always dramatic. Sometimes it's quiet—getting through one more day when you don't want to, putting one foot in front of the other when everything in you wants to quit. Maybe you survived by fighting back, or by going numb, or by finding tiny reasons to keep going when the big reasons weren't enough. Maybe you had help, or maybe you clawed your way out alone. Either way, you made it through something that many people wouldn't have.

What you survived changed you. You're not the same person who went into that experience, and you can't pretend to be. Maybe you're harder now, or softer, or both depending on the day. Maybe you have scars—physical or emotional—that won't ever fully heal. Maybe you're stronger, or maybe you're just tired. Maybe you're grateful to be alive, or maybe you're still processing what it cost you to survive.

The story of what you survived isn't about inspiration or redemption. It's about truth. It's about what happened, how you got through it, and who you became on the other side. This is the story of the thing that almost broke you, and how you're still standing anyway.

Writing Prompt Questions

1. What did you survive? You don't have to share every detail, but what was the experience that tested whether you'd make it through? What were you up against?

2. How did you survive it? What got you through—fight, numbness, help from others, sheer stubbornness? What kept you going when quitting seemed easier?

3. Was there a moment when you thought you wouldn't make it? A rock bottom, a breaking point, a day you weren't sure you'd survive? What was that moment like?

4. Who showed up for you during that time, and who didn't? Were there people who surprised you by staying or leaving? How did their presence or absence affect your survival?

5. How did surviving that experience change you? Are you stronger, angrier, softer, more guarded? What's different about you now because of what you survived?

6. Looking back, what do you want people to understand about survival? What do you know now that you didn't know before, and what would you tell someone going through something similar?

The Regret

"In the end, we only regret the chances we didn't take."
— Lewis Carroll

Most regrets aren't about the things you did—they're about the things you didn't do. The risks you didn't take, the words you didn't say, the person you didn't fight for, the opportunity you let slip away because you were scared or practical or convinced there'd be another chance. But there wasn't another chance, or if there was, it wasn't the same. And now you carry that regret, wondering what would have happened if you'd been braver, bolder, or just willing to try.

Maybe your regret is about a relationship—the person you should have told you loved them, or the one you should have left sooner, or the apology you never made. Maybe it's about a career move you didn't take, a place you didn't go, a dream you didn't pursue because life got in the way or fear won. Maybe it's about your kids—time you didn't spend, words you wish you'd said, moments you can't get back. Or maybe it's something you did do, a choice you made that you'd take back if you could.

Regret has weight. It sits with you in quiet moments, surfaces when you see someone else doing the thing you didn't do, or when you wonder how your life would be different if you'd chosen differently. Some regrets fade over time. Others stay sharp, a reminder of the gap between who you are and who you could have been if you'd made a different choice.

This isn't about beating yourself up—it's about honesty. About naming the thing you wish you'd done differently and acknowledging what it cost you not to do it. Maybe you've made peace with it, or maybe you're still carrying it. Either way, this is the story of the choice you wish you could take back, or the chance you wish you'd taken.

Writing Prompt Questions

1. What's your biggest regret? What choice did you make (or not make) that you wish you could go back and change? What happened, or didn't happen, because of that choice?

2. What stopped you from doing what you wish you'd done? Fear, practicality, someone's opinion, circumstances? What held you back?

3. When did you realize you regretted it? Was it immediate, or did it dawn on you years later? What triggered the realization that you'd made the wrong choice?

4. How has that regret affected your life? Does it surface often, or only occasionally? Does it change how you make decisions now?

5. Have you tried to fix it, make amends, or revisit that choice? If yes, how did that go? If no, what stops you from trying?

6. If you could talk to your younger self at the moment of that decision, what would you say? Would you tell yourself to do it differently, or do you understand now why you made the choice you did?

The Apology

"An apology is the superglue of life. It can repair just about anything."
— Lynn Johnston

There's a difference between the apologies you don't owe and the ones you should have given but didn't. Maybe pride got in the way, or stubbornness, or the belief that you were right and they were wrong so why should you be the one to apologize. Maybe too much time passed and it started to feel too late, too awkward, too complicated to bring up again. Or maybe you just convinced yourself it didn't matter, that they'd moved on, that an apology wouldn't change anything anyway. But you know better. You know there's someone out there you hurt, and you never said you were sorry.

The person might have been a friend you wronged, a partner you treated badly, a family member you lashed out at, or someone you betrayed in a moment of selfishness or anger. Maybe what you did seemed justified at the time—you were hurt, they deserved it, you were protecting yourself. But looking back now, you can see it differently. You can see where you were wrong, where you caused harm, where an apology was owed and never given.

What stops you from apologizing now? Maybe they're no longer in your life and you don't know how to reach them. Maybe you're afraid they won't accept it, or that bringing it up will make things worse. Maybe your ego still resists admitting you were wrong. Or maybe you're just scared—of their reaction, of reopening old wounds, of having to face what you did and own it out loud.

The apology you should have made sits with you differently than other regrets. It's not about a missed opportunity—it's about a debt unpaid, a wound you caused that never got tended to. This is the story of who you hurt and why you never said sorry.

Writing Prompt Questions

1. Who do you owe an apology to, and what did you do? What happened between you that hurt them, and why didn't you apologize at the time?

2. What stopped you from apologizing when it happened? Pride, anger, the belief that you were justified? What kept those words from coming out of your mouth?

3. When did you realize you should have apologized? Was it immediate, or did it take years for you to see it differently? What changed your perspective?

4. Have you thought about apologizing now, even after all this time? What stops you—fear, embarrassment, not knowing how to reach them, or believing it's too late?

5. If you could apologize now, what would you say? Not the defensive version, but the real, honest apology they deserved then and might still deserve now?

6. How has not apologizing affected you? Does it weigh on you, or have you made peace with it? What would giving that apology—even now—do for you or for them?

Failing Forward

"Ever tried. Ever failed. No matter. Try again. Fail again. Fail better."
— Samuel Beckett

Failure isn't gentle. It doesn't tap you on the shoulder and politely inform you that things didn't work out. It crashes in loud and unmistakable—the business that tanked, the test you bombed, the relationship that imploded, the gamble that didn't pay off. You put yourself out there, gave it everything you had, and it still didn't work. Maybe people saw it happen. Maybe you had to admit it out loud. Maybe the evidence of your failure was impossible to hide or spin into something prettier.

The worst part about failing spectacularly isn't just that you failed—it's that you cared. You wanted it to work. You believed it would. You ignored the warning signs or pushed through them because you were convinced you could make it happen through sheer force of will. And when it all came crashing down, you couldn't pretend you hadn't tried. Everyone knew you'd swung for the fences and missed.

Spectacular failures stay with you differently than small ones. They're the stories that make you cringe years later, the memories that still sting a little when they surface. But they're also the ones that taught you the most—about your limits, about resilience, about what happens when you dust yourself off and keep going anyway. You learned who stayed when things got ugly and who disappeared. You learned what you're made of when everything falls apart.

Some failures are quiet lessons. Others are loud, public, undeniable reminders that you're human. This is one of the loud ones, and what it taught you about surviving the aftermath. Maybe it redirected you toward something better, or maybe it just proved you could get knocked down and still get back up. Either way, you failed forward, and that counts for something.

Writing Prompt Questions

1. What did you fail at, and how badly did it go? Set the scene: what were you trying to do, how much did you invest (time, money, emotion), and when did you realize it wasn't going to work?

2. How public was the failure? Did everyone know, or was it something you could hide? What was it like having to face people who knew you'd failed?

3. What was the moment you knew it was over? Was there a specific instant when you realized there was no saving it, or did it dawn on you gradually?

4. Looking back now, what did that failure teach you that success never could have? How did it change you, redirect you, or prepare you for something you didn't see coming?

5. How did you handle it in the immediate aftermath? Did you fall apart, get angry, go numb, pretend it was fine? What did you do in the days right after?

6. Who showed up for you (or didn't) when you failed? Were you surprised by who stayed or who disappeared? What did their response teach you about relationships?

Sweet Revenge

"Living well is the best revenge."
— George Herbert

Revenge has a bad reputation, but sometimes it's not about being petty—it's about justice. Someone wronged you, hurt you, or thought they could get away with something, and you decided they weren't going to. Maybe it was calculated and cold, or maybe it was impulsive and hot. Maybe it was dramatic, or maybe it was so subtle they didn't even realize it was happening. Either way, you evened the score, and it felt good.

The best revenge stories aren't always about destruction. Sometimes it's about proving someone wrong who underestimated you. Sometimes it's about succeeding after they tried to hold you back. Sometimes it's about letting them see exactly what they lost when they mistreated you. And sometimes, yes, it's about making sure they felt a fraction of what they made you feel. Not because you're cruel, but because fairness demanded it.

Maybe you got revenge on an ex who cheated, a boss who mistreated you, a friend who betrayed you, or someone who thought you were too weak or too nice to fight back. Maybe you waited months or years for the right moment. Maybe it happened immediately. Maybe they knew it was you, or maybe they never connected the dots. Either way, when it was done, there was a satisfaction in knowing you didn't just let it go—you handled it.

People will tell you revenge is beneath you, that you should take the high road. But sometimes the high road is making sure people don't get away with hurting you. And that's not wrong—that's boundaries with teeth. This is the story of who wronged you, what you did about it, and whether evening the score gave you the closure you were looking for.

Writing Prompt Questions

1. Who wronged you, and what did they do that made you decide they deserved payback? What was the offense, and why couldn't you just let it go?

2. How did you plan your revenge—was it premeditated, or did the opportunity just present itself? Walk through how you decided what to do and when to do it.

3. What did you actually do? Describe the revenge itself—was it public or private, subtle or obvious, immediate or delayed?

4. Did they know it was you, or did you stay anonymous? If they knew, how did they react? If they didn't, what was it like watching them deal with the consequences without knowing who caused them?

5. How did it feel when you finally got your revenge? Satisfying? Anticlimactic? Did it give you closure, or did it leave you wanting more?

6. Do you regret it, or would you do it again? Looking back, was the revenge justified, or do you wish you'd handled it differently? Did it make things better or just even?

About the Author

Jed Smith is a father, musician, writer, and digital entrepreneur. After twenty years in the building material supply industry, he shifted gears and founded TorchOwl Library—a publishing house exploring the intersection between ancient human wisdom and modern intelligence.

TorchOwl publishes across five core areas: Healing & Manifestation, Fundamental Knowledge and Skills, Relationships, Communication and the Arts, and Professional Development. Each publication helps readers engage with what makes humanity beautiful—connection, creativity, resilience, and authentic self-expression.

The philosophy driving TorchOwl is simple: technology should enhance our humanity, not replace it. By leveraging AI and digital tools thoughtfully, TorchOwl creates resources that make space for people to explore deeper aspects of life. The goal isn't to optimize people into productivity machines, but to provide tools that help them become more fully themselves.

Jed's songwriting workbook became a #1 new release in multiple categories, reflecting his belief that creativity and self-expression are fundamental to human flourishing. The Badass Mom Story Journal represents TorchOwl's commitment to authentic storytelling and legacy preservation—addressing mothers who've lived unconventionally and have stories worth preserving exactly as they happened, unfiltered and unapologetic.

Above all, Jed loves being a dad. His children inspire him to create resources that help people preserve what matters, express what's real, and leave something meaningful behind.

Thank you for your interest in...

The Badass Mom Guided Story Journal

If you enjoyed this journal, an honest review would be appreciated.

Thank you for taking a moment to share your experience.

- Jed Smith

Made in the USA
Coppell, TX
13 February 2026